INSIGHT POCKET GUIDE

SWITZE

Discovery CHANNEL

APA PUBLICATIONS
Part of the Langenscheidt Publishing Group

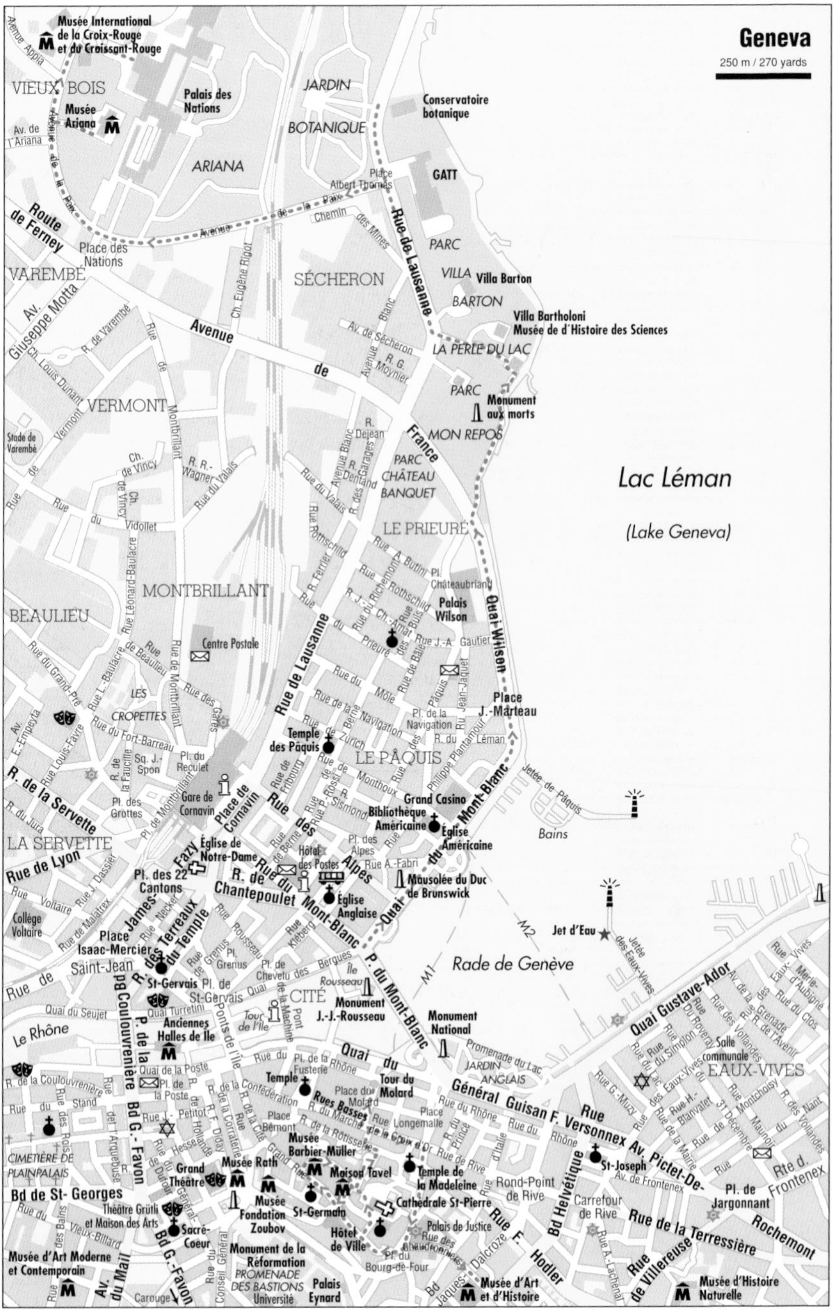

Geneva
250 m / 270 yards
Musée International de la Croix-Rouge et du Croissant-Rouge
Avenue Appia
VIEUX BOIS
Musée Ariana
Av. de l'Ariana
Avenue de la Paix
Palais des Nations
ARIANA
JARDIN
BOTANIQUE
Conservatoire botanique
Place Albert Thomas
GATT
Chemin des Mines
Rue de Lausanne
PARC
VILLA
BARTON
Villa Barton
Villa Bartholoni Musée de d'Histoire des Sciences
LA PERLE DU LAC
PARC
MON REPOS
Monument aux morts
Route de Ferney
Place des Nations
VAREMBÉ
SÉCHERON
Ch. Eugène Rigot
Av. Giuseppe Motta
R. de Varembé
Ch. Louis Dunant
Avenue de France
Av. de Sécheron
R. G. Moynier
Avenue Blanc
VERMONT
Stade de Varembé
Rue de Vermont
Rue de Montbrillant
R. Dejean
Ch. de Vincy
R. R.-Wagner
Rue du Valais
Rue du Vidollet
Avenue Blanc
R. des Garages
R. Dentand
PARC CHÂTEAU BANQUET
Lac Léman
(Lake Geneva)
LE PRIEURÉ
Rue Rothschild
R. Ferrier
Rue A. Butin
Pl. Châteaubriand
Rue du Richemont
Rue Rothschild
Rue des Buis
R. J.-Ch.-Amat
Palais Wilson
Quai Wilson
MONTBRILLANT
BEAULIEU
Rue Léonard-Baulacre
Centre Postale
Rue de Lausanne
Rue du Prieuré
Rue J.-A. Gautier
Rue de Bâle
Rue des Pâquis
Ru. Jean-Jaquet
Place J.-Marteau
Rue du Grand-Pré
Rue L.-Baulacre
Rue de Beaulieu
LES CROPETTES
Rue des Gares
Rue du Môle
Rue de la Navigation
Pl. de la Navigation
R. du Léman
Philippe Plantamour
Av. E.-Empeyta
Rue du Fort-Barreau
Rue Louis-Favre
R. de la Faucille
Sq. J.-Spon
Pl. du Reculet
Rue de Berne
Rue de Zurich
Temple des Pâquis
LE PÂQUIS
R. de la Servette
R. du Jura
Pl. des Grottes
Gare de Cornavin
Place de Cornavin
Rue des Alpes
Rue de Fribourg
Rue de Monthoux
R. Sismondi
Grand Casino
Bibliothèque Américaine
Église Américaine
Quai du Mont-Blanc
Jetée de Pâquis
Bains
LA SERVETTE
Rue de Lyon
Rue J. Dassier
Rue Voltaire
Collège Voltaire
Église de Notre-Dame
Pl. des 22 Cantons
R. de Chantepoulet
Rue Fazy
Hôtel des Postes
Pl. des Alpes
Rue A.-Fabri
Mausolée du Duc de Brunswick
Église Anglaise
R. du Mont-Blanc
Jet d'Eau
Jetée des Eaux-Vives
M1
M2
Rade de Genève
Rue de Malatrex
Place Isaac-Mercier
James-Fazy
Rue Necker
R. des Terreaux du Temple
Rue Rousseau
Rue Kléberg
Rue de Saint-Jean
St-Gervais
Pl. de St-Gervais
Rue des Grenus
Pl. Grenus
Pl. de Chevelu
Quai des Bergues
Île Rousseau
P. du Mont-Blanc
Monument J.-J.-Rousseau
Monument National
CITÉ
Quai du Seujet
Le Rhône
Bd de la Coulouvrenière
Anciennes Halles de l'Île
Tour de l'Île
Pont de la Machine
Ponts de l'Île
P. de la Coulouvrenière
Quai de la Poste
Pl. de la Poste
Rue du Rhône
Pl. de la Fusterie
Temple
Place du Molard
Tour du Molard
Quai du Général Guisan
Promenade du Lac
JARDIN ANGLAIS
Quai Gustave-Ador
Salle communale
EAUX-VIVES
Rue des Vollandes
Rue de la Grenade
Rue du Clos
R. de l'Avenir
Rue du Simplon
Rue du Lac
Rue des Eaux-Vives
Rue G.-Muzy
Rue H.-Blanvalet
Rue du 31 Décembre
Rue de Montchoisy
Rue Maunoir
R. des Vollandes
Rue du Nant
R. de la Coulouvrenière
Rue du Stand
Rue de l'Arquebuse
Bd G.-Favon
Rue J.-Petitot
Rue de Hollande
R. de la Confédération
Rue de la Corraterie
Place Bémont
Rues Basses
R. du Marché
R. de la Rôtisserie
Rue de la Croix-d'Or
Rue Longemalle
Place Longemalle
R. du Prince
Rue du Rhône
Rue d'Italie
Rue F. Versonnex
Av. Pictet-De-Rochemont
St-Joseph
Av. de Frontenex
Rte d. Frontenex
CIMETIÈRE DE PLAINPALAIS
Rue des Rois
Rue Hesse
Rue du Général-Dufour
R. Diday
Grand Théâtre
Musée Rath
Musée Barbier-Müller
Maison Tavel
Temple de la Madeleine
Rue de Rive
Rond-Point de Rive
Carrefour de Rive
Bd Helvétique
Pl. de Jargonnant
Bd de St-Georges
Théâtre Grütli et Maison des Arts
Rue du Vieux-Billard
Rue des Bains
Musée Fondation Zoubov
St-Germain
Cathédrale St-Pierre
Palais de Justice
Rue des Chaudronniers
Rue F. Hodler
Rue de la Terrassière
Rue A.-Lachenal
Rue de Villereuse
Sacré-Coeur
Hôtel de Ville
Pl. du Bourg-de-Four
Musée d'Art Moderne et Contemporain
Monument de la Réformation
PROMENADE DES BASTIONS
Université
Palais Eynard
Bd Jaques-Dalcroze
Musée d'Art et d'Histoire
Musée d'Histoire Naturelle
Av. du Mail
Carouge
Rue du Conseil Général

Welcome

This guidebook combines the interests and enthusiasms of two of the world's best-known information providers: Insight Guides, who have set the standard for visual travel guides since 1970, and Discovery Channel, the world's premier source of non-fiction television programming. Its aim is to select the best of Switzerland in a series of tailor-made itineraries devised by one of Insight's correspondents in the country, Vivien Stone.

The 15 itineraries in the book provide something to suit all tastes, budgets and trip lengths. As well as Switzerland's classic destinations there are details on lesser known sights and carefully planned suggestions for those who want to extend their visit to particular regions or take time out for some of the outdoor pursuits, such as hiking and skiing, for which the country is so well known. So if you are keen to tour the country's beautifully preserved old towns, sail on the crystal-clear lakes, hike in the majestic Alps or simply sample the French, German, Italian and Romansh cultural tapestry that makes up the country, you will find itineraries to suit. They are set in context by an introductory history section and supported by plenty of specific suggestions on accommodation, restaurants, shopping, activities and the practicalities of getting around and making the most of your trip.

Vivien Stone has a great deal of experience of the travel guide genre, being a writer, a reader and, formerly, the editorial director of a major guide book series. She is keen to share her knowledge of Switzerland, which she has been getting to know over the past five years. 'With beautiful mountain peaks, pretty alpine villages and medieval towns filled with a variety of French, German and Italian influences, it's a mosaic of a country both culturally and geographically, which makes it a fascinating place to visit,' she says. 'It has been fun to present not only the classic destinations of the country, such as Bern, with its arcaded medieval old town, and the magical setting of Zermatt crowned by the mighty Matterhorn, but to include itineraries to some of the lesser-known places, such as the picturesque towns along the Rhine in the far north of the country and the Romansh-speaking Engadine Valley in the far east.'

contents

History and Culture

Itineraries

These 15 excursions, of up to three days' duration, cover all of the country's essential sights. All incorporate travel, accommodation and restaurant tips.

Leisure Activities

Calendar of Events

Practical Information

Maps

Index and Credits

Pages 2/3: the resort of Zermatt
Pages 8/9: Rauthausplatz, Stein am Rhein

upp + Cie
Restaurant
zum
Roten Ochsen

History & Culture

The history of Switzerland is one of a remarkable union of some very disparate elements over many centuries. In great contrast to the pastoral, peace-loving image the country enjoys today, its early history is one of struggle and bloodshed. In many ways it is a country that learned the benefits of consensus and the folly of territorial ambitions long before many of its European neighbours. On the downside, in recent years the country's squeaky clean human rights image has been tarnished by revelations of its political and economic dealings during World War II, and social ills such as racism and drug problems do not stop at Switzerland's borders.

Early History

People were known to have been living on the plains and in stilt villages around the lakes of northern and western Switzerland around 12000BC. Caves in the Jura, where human bones dating back 50,000 years have been found, may have been the sites of even earlier settlements. By 200BC Celtic peoples from France, the Helvetii, had moved into western Switzerland though they were held back from expanding their territory by Germanic tribes to the north and east. After Julius Caesar (101–44BC) won the battle of Bribacte (in modern Burgundy), the Romans established their empire over much of modern-day Switzerland. Early settlements date to 58BC, after which Geneva, Nyon, Martigny, Avenches, Baden, Chur and Zürich became thriving Roman towns. By the end of the 3rd century AD, however, the Alemanni tribe from north of the Rhine had moved into northern and central Switzerland and by AD 400 had crushed what remained of Roman rule.

It wasn't long before the Alemanni were themselves under threat from the Franks, a dynasty that encouraged the spread of Christianity and the development of monasteries. The abbey of St Gallen was founded in 614 by an Irish missionary, Gallus, who was a follower of St Colomba. In 800, Charlemagne, king of the Franks, was crowned emperor of what was to become the Holy Roman Empire. Following his death in 814, Switzerland split into two parts – the west became part of the kingdom of Burgundy, the centre and north returned to the control of the Alemanni.

By the mid-11th century the whole region was united under the Holy Roman Empire. Within the loose control exercised by the emperor over Swiss territory, some powerful dynasties, most notably the Zähringen, Savoy and Habsburg families, gained control of large areas of land and wealth to the extent that they were given dispensation to found cities such as Bern (1191). Feudal law reigned and there were frequent conflicts as the powerful families battled to retain or extend their land and influence. Many

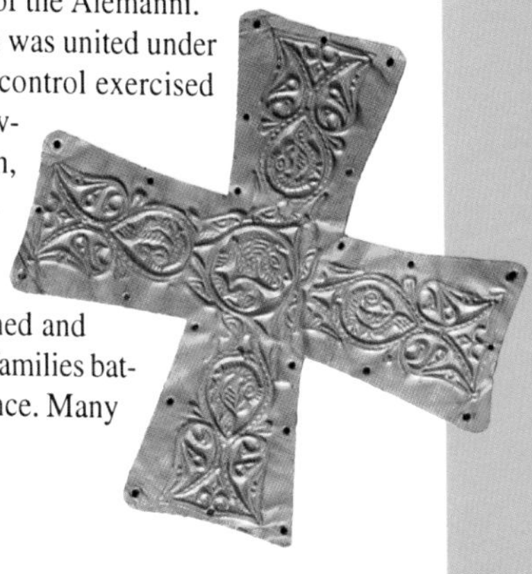

Left: the legacy of ancient Rome
Right: 7th-century Lombard Cross

towns were founded for strategic reasons, often to shore up defences against rival powers. In the early 13th century the Zähringen family line came to an end and the houses of Savoy and Habsburg competed for the spoils. The Duke of Savoy took control of Geneva and the area around the lake, and the Habsburgs took much of the rest. Rudolf I of Habsburg was crowned Holy Roman Emperor in 1273.

The Swiss Confederation

The Gotthard Pass opened in the early years of the 13th century. This new thoroughfare greatly increased the importance of the northern cantons at a time when they were objecting to the rule of local lords and bailiffs imposed by the Holy Roman Empire. As a result, the three forest cantons of Schwyz, Uri and Unterwalden forged an alliance in 1291. According to legend, local leaders swore an oath in a field called Rütli Meadow near Brunnen. This is marked in history (and by the annual National Day celebrations on August 1) as the start of the Swiss Confederation, which a total of 26 cantons would join in the following centuries. The event's historic hallmarks – the strength of mutual alliance, the power of consensus and the benefits of co-operation – became values to which Swiss political groups have aspired ever since.

After the death of Rudolf I in 1291, the Holy Roman Empire in Switzerland began to wane. The legend of William Tell, with its theme of a local citizen resisting the feudal overlord, relates to this time. Such tales can be found elsewhere in Europe but in Switzerland, constant retelling of the William Tell story – and, since the 19th century, the popularity of Schiller's play and Rossini's opera – have resulted in the myth being viewed more as history.

Within a century the powerful cantons of Lucerne, Zürich and Bern had joined the confederation. During this time Swiss soldiers, regarded as Europe's best, were used as mercenaries in far-flung European conflicts. Some of the beautiful mansions of central Switzerland, in Schwyz for example, attest to the wealth to be made from this profession, which continued to be important into the 18th century.

The 15th century saw both St Gallen and lands south of the Alps – the Ticino – come under the aegis of the confederation. Charles the Bold of Burgundy was defeated at Grandson in 1476 by the Swiss, marking the end of the rule of the dukes of Burgundy and their hopes of establishing a kingdom stretching from the Low Countries to the Mediterranean. The victorious Swiss carried off treasure that became known as the 'Burgundian booty', some of which can today be seen in the Bern Historical Museum. By 1513, the cantons of Basel and Appenzell had joined the confederation, and the Swiss parliament (Diet) met regularly. Tensions were on the rural-urban and Catholic-Protestant lines that were to divide much of Europe for centuries to come.

Left: William Tell is a national hero

The Reformation

It was at this time that the Reformation, sparked by the ideas of Martin Luther, took hold in Switzerland, causing violent upheavals in the religious and political life of the country. Ulrich Zwingli was the first significant Swiss Reformation figure; from his base in Zürich he preached the new Protestant doctrine and urged puritanical reforms, including the removal of pictures and images from the churches. The city guilds were in favour of the reforms, which laid emphasis on hard work and sobriety – laying the foundations for an image of Switzerland that abides to this day, of hard work and inconspicuous wealth. The Catholic forest cantons refused to convert; bloody battles ensued and, in 1531, Zwingli was killed. A little later in the 16th century Jean Calvin in Geneva and Guillame Farel in Neuchâtel took up the cause. Calvin died in 1564 having made Geneva as synonymous with Protestantism as Rome is with Catholicism. From this time, many Swiss cities became the refuge of persecuted Protestants from Italy and France, notably Huguenots, who brought with them traditions of jewellery-making and silk weaving that ultimately gave rise to today's huge watch-making and pharmaceuticals industries in Switzerland.

Tensions within the country between Protestant and Catholic cantons continued, with the wealthy Protestant cities usually retaining the upper hand. Beyond its borders, however, Switzerland's reputation for neutrality was officially first recognised following the Thirty Years' War, which engulfed much of the rest of central Europe from 1618 to 1648. War – beyond its frontier – was profitable, as Switzerland had discovered with the high price commanded by its mercenaries, and the economy did well from the export of foodstuffs and the flow of skilled refugees into its towns.

After the Thirty Years' War ended, the area making up the confederation was officially recognised as an independent state. Despite this international acceptance, Switzerland's internal tensions continued, and it wasn't until 1712, with the Peace of Aargau, that the violent religious conflict ended and Protestants and Catholics were able to live in a spirit of tolerance.

Above: Calvin delivers a parting lecture from his deathbed

In 1798, following the French Revolution, Napoleon invaded. His forces conquered Bern, and he established the Helvetic Republic. In an attempt to create a unified state he took power away from the individual cantons. This was in complete opposition to the way the Swiss had governed themselves for centuries and, within four years, Napoleon's troops were forced to leave. There followed a period during which the autonomous power of the cantons was re-established to some degree but it wasn't until 1815 and the defeat of Napoleon at Waterloo that they regained full control of their affairs.

Switzerland in the 19th Century

The period between 1830 and 1848 is known as the Sonderbund War. The old problem of religious prejudices and the resulting imposition of economic disadvantages continued to beset the predominantly Protestant towns and the less developed Catholic cantons. As a result, the Catholic cantons formed the Sonderbund or Separatist League to defy the power of the big cities. In a decisive move to negate the threat of a potentially long and disastrous civil war, Henri Dufour led the Swiss army to a rapid victory over the Catholic forces in 1847. The following year, one of revolutions across Europe, the entire country adopted a federal constitution and a central government was set up in Bern, which became the capital of the Swiss Confederation. The genuinely federal power structure and liberal policies promulgated by the constitution are still in force today, and the individual regional cantons still enjoy considerable political and economic power. The country was further democratised in 1874, when the referendum was adopted as the main method of decision-making for national policies.

The latter half of the 19th century was a period of considerable economic growth and social stability. An impressive railway network started to take shape, numerous banks were founded and significant industries such as textiles were mechanised. Agriculture became more commercialised, with an emphasis on dairy products and beef (as opposed to cereals that could be grown much more cheaply elsewhere). Food-processing industries such

Above: Zürich in Zwingli's day

as the manufacture of cheese and chocolate grew in importance, and Swiss products started to be exported in large quantities.

The scene-stealing natural beauty of the country also began to draw large numbers of foreign visitors, especially the British. In the early days of tourism the country was primarily a summer destination, but in the second half of the 19th century the appreciation of snow-filled landscapes, and activities such as skiing, took off. Thomas Cook, the Victorian travel agent, organised his first package holiday to Switzerland in 1863. The tour took in the now classic itinerary of Lake Geneva, the sights along the Rhône valley (the Valais) and up into Interlaken and the Jungfrau massif. Switzerland's clean mountain air became a fashionable prescription and many patients, particularly those with chest-related complaints such as tuberculosis, were sent to recuperate in the mountains and the lakeside clinics and resorts that began to spring up towards the end of the 19th century.

Henri Dunant founded the International Red Cross in 1864, thereby marking the start of Switzerland's eager participation in international humanitarian affairs. Moved by the appalling carnage between French and Italian troops that he witnessed at the Battle of Solferino in 1859, Dunant lobbied for the creation of a neutral organisation that could care for those wounded in war. In 1864 the first Geneva Convention was ratified by 16 countries and the International Red Cross was founded. In 1901 Dunant was awarded the Nobel Peace prize for his pioneering work.

World Wars

Switzerland retained its neutral status during World War I, though it is widely acknowledged that, for much of the conflict, the sympathies of the mainly German-speaking army lay with Germany. Following the war the League of Nations was established in 1919, with its headquarters in Geneva.

Switzerland's neutrality during World War II was tempered with a good deal of political and economic expediency. Surrounded on all sides by the Axis powers, Switzerland came to a number of agreements to avoid being invaded – a very real threat in the early years of the war. The Gotthard Tunnel, for example, remained open to the German forces and was a key link with their allies in Italy. The Swiss economy fared well during the war, as the country supplied equipment and foodstuffs to both sides, and large amounts of money flowed into Swiss banks for safe-keeping.

Switzerland's attitudes to the victims of Nazi oppression – the Jews and other minorities in Germany and occupied Europe – has, over the past few years, come in for much scrutiny and criticism. The fanatically secret Swiss banks have had to open up and admit the scale of the funds accepted from the German exchequer and from Holocaust victims. In the late 1990s, after years of refusal to acknowledge the problem, Swiss banks finally accepted that many of the long-standing claims were financially and morally significant; the banks agreed to offer large sums of money in settlement to the

Right: bust of Henri Dunant at the Red Cross Museum

victims and their relatives, many of whom were by then in extreme old age. In 1995 Kaspar Villiger, the Swiss president, apologised for the lack of humanitarian assistance offered by Switzerland to refugees attempting to flee occupied Europe. Shamingly, and in complete opposition to the humanitarian face Switzerland likes to portray to the world, it became common knowledge that, in 1938, Switzerland requested that the Germans introduce a 'J' stamp in the passports of German Jews.

United Nations Headquarters

In 1946, Geneva became the European headquarters of the United Nations. The city has since attracted lots of international (trade, aid, wildlife, religious) agencies. The Swiss franc has long been a stable currency, and Swiss banks and insurance companies have a reputation for financial expertise. In 1992 Switzerland voted to stay out of the European Union, but it is an increasingly international country. Most of its people speak more than one language and English is becoming the second language of the younger generation.

Switzerland has seen its foreign population rise considerably over the past few decades; today more than 20 percent of the working population is non-Swiss. In Geneva this is considerably higher, at around 40 percent. This diverse body of foreign workers is found particularly in the finance, pharmaceuticals and technology sectors, in the international organisations and as guest workers who are welcomed to fill some of the jobs the Swiss would rather not do themselves – domestic and agricultural labour and low-paid service sector employment, such as in restaurants. Despite an openness to all these outside influences and its very central geographical position in Europe, at the heart of Swiss life there remains an undeniably strong strain of conservatism – as is shown by the very late date (1971) at which women won the right to vote in national elections. Traditional family life and structures are respected and huge subsidies are pumped into maintaining that symbol of the country, traditional valley agriculture. Overall though, Switzerland continues to be a mosaic of very different components that constitutes a fine, if rather perplexing, whole.

History Highlights

12000BC Evidence of settlements in the north and west of the country.
200BC The Helvetii, a Celtic tribe, settle in western Switzerland.
58BC Roman settlements founded in the west and south of Switzerland. Roman infrastructure established, including the Grand St Bernard Pass.
AD260 Germanic tribes start to colonise much of Switzerland beyond the west.
400 The Roman empire in Switzerland collapses.
614 St Gallen founded by the Irish monk Gallus.
814 Death of Charlemagne; Switzerland splits in two.
834 Treaty of Verdun – Burgundy rules the western part of Switzerland; the Teutonic Alemannians take the rest.
12th century Habsburg, Zähringen and Savoy families establish feudal rule over much of the country.
1191 Duke of Zähringen founds Bern.
1220 Gotthard Pass between northern Europe and the Mediterranean opens.
1291 Pact of mutual support sworn by the cantons of Schwyz, Uri and Unterwalden in Rütli Meadow marks the start of the Swiss Confederation.
1332 Lucerne joins the confederation.
1351 Zürich joins the confederation.
1388 The confederation numbers eight cantons, including Bern.
15th century Ticino and St Gallen are taken by Swiss confederates.
1476 Swiss troops defeat Charles the Bold of Burgundy.
1513 The confederation numbers 13 cantons. The Diet holds regular meetings; decisions made by consensus.
16th century The Reformation.
1531 Ulrich Zwingli killed.
1536 Calvin preaches in Geneva.
1648 Switzerland's neutrality during the Thirty Years' War is recognised.
1712 The Peace of Aargau ends the violent struggle between Protestants and Catholics.
18th century Age of Enlightenment: Rousseau's ideas take root.
1798 Napoleon invades, takes Bern, and establishes the Helvetic Republic.
1815 Napoleon is defeated at Waterloo and the Helvetic Republic collapses. The confederation numbers 22 cantons.
1830–48 Civil war between Catholic and Protestant cantons. Henri Dufour crushes Catholic resistance in 1847.
1848 A secular federal constitution adopted. Bern becomes the capital and a central government is established.
1863 First Thomas Cook tour.
1864 The first Geneva Convention is ratified by 16 countries; International Red Cross is founded.
1874 The referendum becomes the main way to decide national issues.
1914–18 Switzerland officially remains neutral during WWI.
1919 League of Nations is established.
1939–45 Switzerland officially remains neutral during WWII.
1946 United Nations offices established in Geneva.
1971 Women gain the vote in national elections.
1978 The Jura splits from Bern to make 26 cantons.
1992 Swiss vote to stay out of the EU.
1995 Headquarters of the World Trade Organisation established in Geneva. Also in this year, Swiss president apologises for requesting the 'J' stamp be introduced into passports of German Jews in 1938 and for closing its borders to refugees in 1942.
1998 Swiss banks agree to a $1.25 billion settlement for Holocaust claims.
2002 Switzerland joins the United Nations.

Left: signs of multicultural times in Zürich

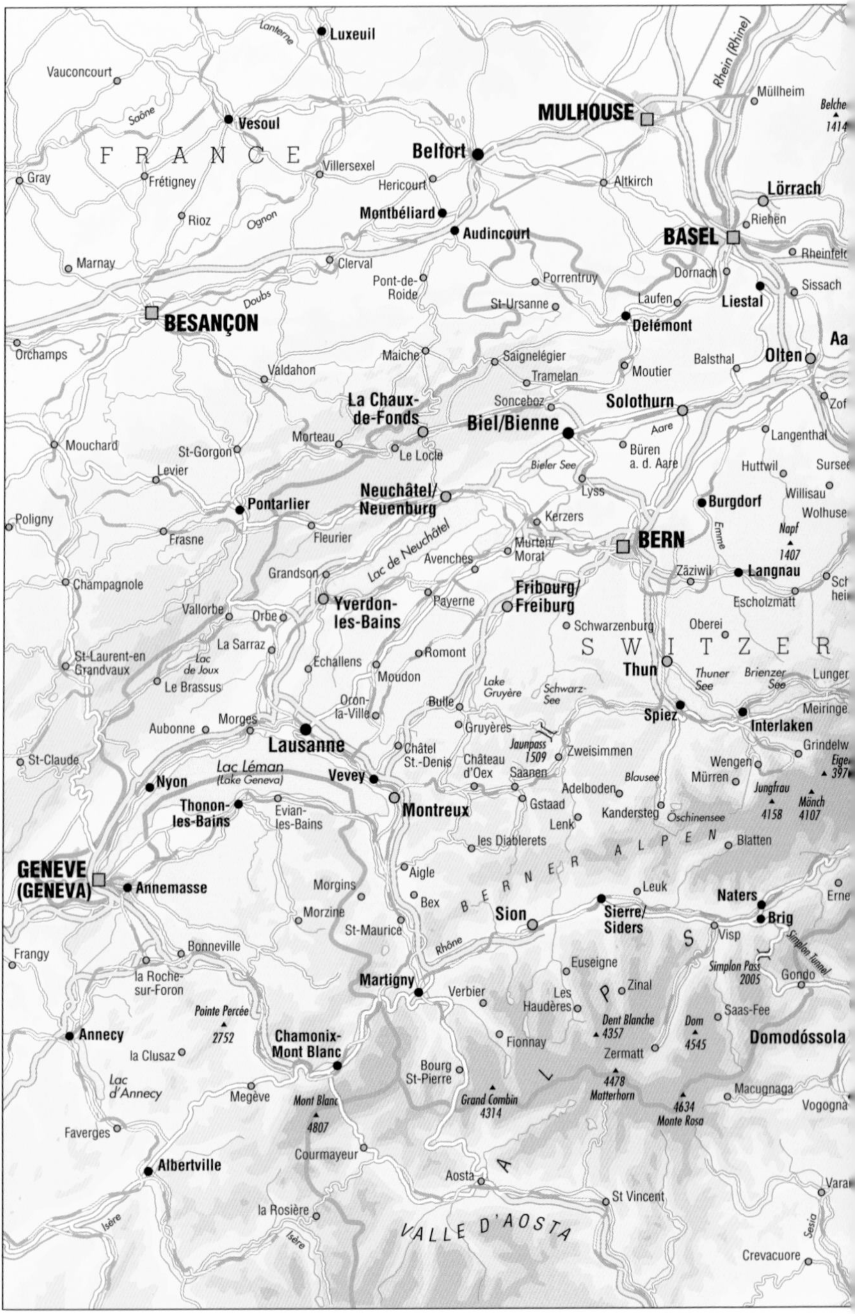
Lanterne
Luxeuil
Vauconcourt
Saône
Vesoul
F R A N C E
Gray
Frétigney
Villersexel
Belfort
MULHOUSE
Rhein (Rhine)
Müllheim
Belche
1414
Hericourt
Altkirch
Lörrach
Riehen
Rioz
Ognon
Montbéliard
Audincourt
BASEL
Rheinfeld
Marnay
Clerval
Pont-de-Roide
Porrentruy
Dornach
Sissach
Liestal
Laufen
St-Ursanne
Doubs
BESANÇON
Delémont
Orchamps
Maiche
Saignelégier
Balsthal
Olten
Aa
Valdahon
Tramelan
Moutier
La Chaux-de-Fonds
Sonceboz
Solothurn
Zof
Biel/Bienne
Aare
Langenthal
Mouchard
Morteau
Le Locle
St-Gorgon
Büren a. d. Aare
Levier
Bieler See
Huttwil
Sursee
Lyss
Neuchâtel/ Neuenburg
Willisau
Pontarlier
Burgdorf
Wolhuse
Poligny
Kerzers
Fleurier
Emme
Napf
1407
Frasne
Murten/ Morat
BERN
Lac de Neuchâtel
Avenches
Grandson
Zäziwil
Langnau
Champagnole
Sch hei
Escholzmatt
Yverdon-les-Bains
Payerne
Fribourg/ Freiburg
Vallorbe
Orbe
Schwarzenburg
Oberei
S W I T Z E R
La Sarraz
Romont
St-Laurent-en Grandvaux
Lac de Joux
Echallens
Thun
Moudon
Thuner See
Brienzer See
Lunger
Le Brassus
Lake Gruyère
Schwarz-See
Oron-la-Ville
Bulle
Spiez
Interlaken
Meiringe
Aubonne
Morges
Gruyères
Lausanne
Jaunpass
1509
Zweisimmen
Grindelw
St-Claude
Châtel St-Denis
Château d'Oex
Saanen
Wengen
Eige
397
Lac Léman
(Lake Geneva)
Vevey
Blausee
Mürren
Nyon
Adelboden
Jungfrau
4158
Mönch
4107
Gstaad
Thonon-les-Bains
Evian-les-Bains
Montreux
Kandersteg
Öschinensee
Lenk
les Diablerets
N
Blatten
B E R N E R A L P E N
GENEVE (GENEVA)
Aigle
Annemasse
Morgins
Leuk
Erne
Bex
Naters
Sion
Sierre/ Siders
Brig
Morzine
St-Maurice
Visp
Simplon Tunnel
Frangy
Bonneville
Rhône
S
Simplon Pass
2005
la Roche-sur-Foron
Euseigne
Gondo
Martigny
Zinal
P
Verbier
Les Haudères
Pointe Percée
2752
Dent Blanche
4357
Saas-Fee
Dom
4545
Annecy
Chamonix-Mont Blanc
Fionnay
Domodóssola
la Clusaz
Zermatt
L
Bourg St-Pierre
4478
Matterhorn
Lac d'Annecy
Megève
Mont Blanc
4807
Grand Combin
4314
4634
Monte Rosa
Macugnaga
Vogogna
Faverges
Courmayeur
A
Albertville
Aosta
Vara
St Vincent
la Rosière
Isère
VALLE D'AOSTA
Sesia
Crevacuore

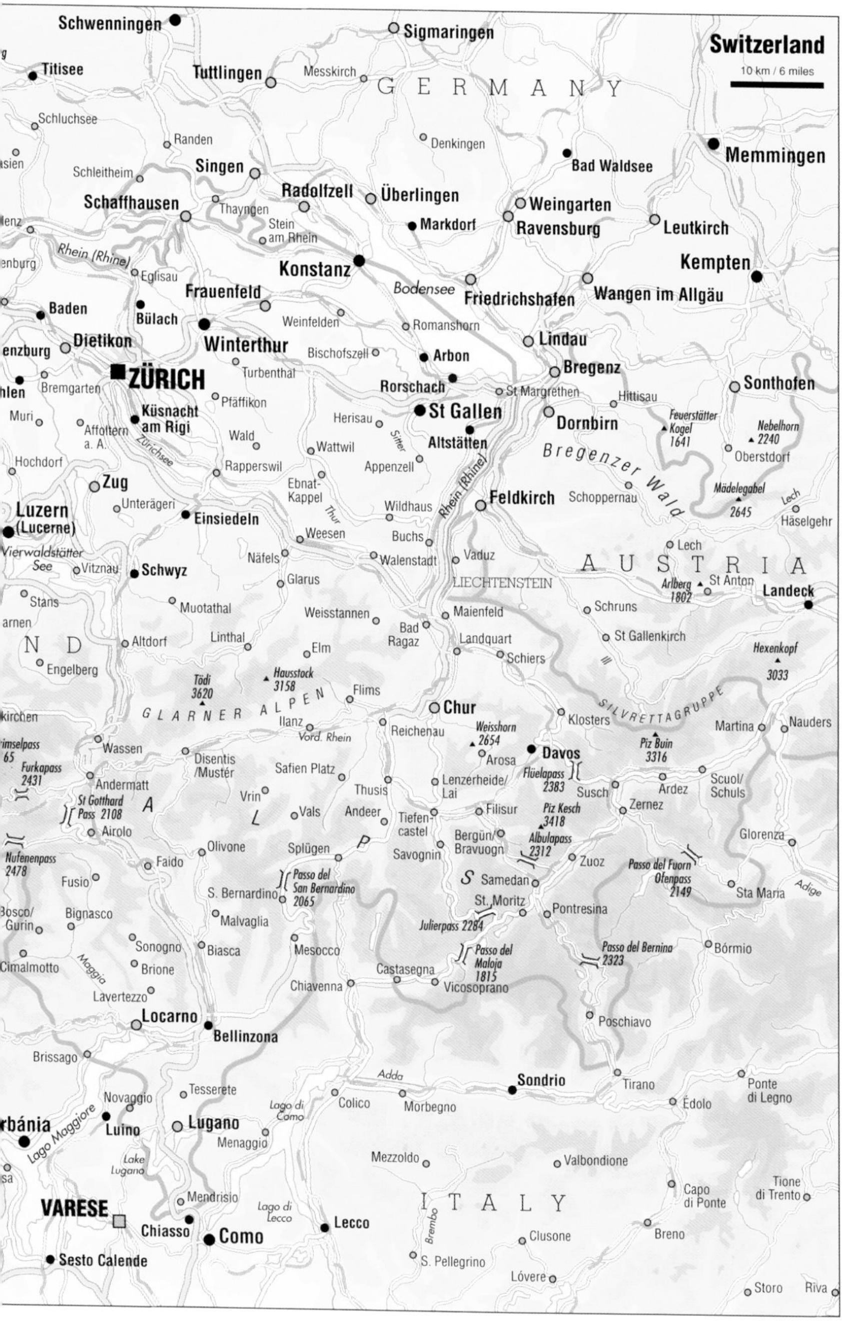

Switzerland
10 km / 6 miles
Schwenningen
Sigmaringen
Titisee
Tuttlingen
Messkirch
GERMANY
Schluchsee
Randen
Denkingen
Memmingen
Bad Waldsee
Schleitheim
Singen
Radolfzell
Überlingen
Schaffhausen
Thayngen
Weingarten
Markdorf
Ravensburg
Leutkirch
Stein am Rhein
Rhein (Rhine)
Konstanz
Kempten
Eglisau
Frauenfeld
Bodensee
Friedrichshafen
Wangen im Allgäu
Baden
Bülach
Weinfelden
Romanshorn
Winterthur
Dietikon
Lindau
Bischofszell
Arbon
Turbenthal
Bregenz
ZÜRICH
Rorschach
Bremgarten
St Margrethen
Hittisau
Sonthofen
Pfäffikon
St Gallen
Küsnacht am Rigi
Herisau
Dornbirn
Feuerstätter Kogel 1641
Nebelhorn 2240
Muri
Affoltern a. A.
Wald
Wattwil
Sitter
Altstätten
Oberstdorf
Zürichsee
Bregenzer Wald
Hochdorf
Rapperswil
Appenzell
Zug
Ebnat-Kappel
Mädelegabel 2645
Unterägeri
Wildhaus
Feldkirch
Schoppernau
Lech
Luzern (Lucerne)
Einsiedeln
Thur
Rhein (Rhine)
Häselgehr
Weesen
Buchs
Lech
Vierwaldstätter See
Vitznau
Schwyz
Näfels
Walenstadt
Vaduz
AUSTRIA
Glarus
LIECHTENSTEIN
Arlberg 1802
St Anton
Landeck
Stans
Muotathal
Weisstannen
Maienfeld
Schruns
Bad Ragaz
St Gallenkirch
Linthal
Landquart
Altdorf
Elm
Schiers
Hexenkopf 3033
Engelberg
Hausstock 3158
Tödi 3620
Flims
GLARNER ALPEN
Chur
SILVRETTAGRUPPE
Ilanz
Klosters
Nauders
Vord. Rhein
Reichenau
Weisshorn 2654
Piz Buin 3316
Martina
Wassen
Disentis /Mustér
Arosa
Davos
Furkapass 2431
Safien Platz
Lenzerheide/ Lai
Flüelapass 2383
Andermatt
Thusis
Susch
Ardez
Scuol/ Schuls
St Gotthard Pass 2108
Vrin
Zernez
Airolo
Vals
Andeer
Tiefen-castel
Filisur
Piz Kesch 3418
ALPS
Glorenza
Nufenenpass 2478
Olivone
Splügen
Bergün/ Bravuogn
Albulapass 2312
Faido
Savognin
Zuoz
Passo del Fuorn Ofenpass 2149
Fusio
Passo del San Bernardino 2065
Samedan
S. Bernardino
Sta Maria
Adige
Bosco/ Gurin
Bignasco
St. Moritz
Pontresina
Malvaglia
Julierpass 2284
Sonogno
Biasca
Mesocco
Passo del Maloja 1815
Passo del Bernina 2323
Bórmio
Cimalmotto
Maggia
Brione
Castasegna
Chiavenna
Vicosoprano
Lavertezzo
Locarno
Bellinzona
Poschiavo
Brissago
Adda
Sondrio
Tesserete
Tirano
Ponte di Legno
Novaggio
Colico
Lago di Como
Morbegno
Édolo
Lago Maggiore
Luino
Lugano
Menaggio
Lake Lugano
Mezzoldo
Valbondione
Mendrisio
ITALY
Capo di Ponte
Tione di Trento
VARESE
Lago di Lecco
Chiasso
Lecco
Como
Brembo
Clusone
Breno
Sesto Calende
S. Pellegrino
Lóvere
Storo
Riva

Western Switzerland

1. Geneva *(see map, p4)*

This whole-day walking tour of Geneva's picturesque hilltop old town takes in some of its historic buildings and a couple of its best museums. The city's main shopping district is conveniently close if you want a break from the cultural sights. For those with another day or two in the city, the chapter incorporates Geneva's more contemporary aspects – lakeside promenades and cruises, the Botanic Gardens, a tour of a United Nations building and the old-fashioned district of Carouge.

Geneva's compact old town is perched on a craggy hill with steep but short lanes running up from the left bank of the lake and the Rue de Rive. Ample cafés and benches make it a manageable tour for all ages. The sights of the right bank are within walking distance of each other, but Carouge, south of the centre, is best reached by tram or bus from the main railway station.

The main square of Geneva's old town, the **Place du Bourg-de-Four**, has long been the area's main meeting point. Take an early morning coffee at La Clémence, in the centre of the square, and soak up the atmosphere and handsome architecture of this one-time Roman forum, medieval market square, gathering place for the Protestant reformer Calvin and his followers, and a stop on the old coaching route. Among the striking buildings is the 18th-century Palais de Justice. The flower-decked fountain gives a clue to another of the square's ancient functions, that of water supply for the old city. Today, the small galleries, antique shops and numerous cafés and restaurants offer plenty of reasons for people to congregate in this historic heart of the city.

The Old Town

Take the Rue de l'Hôtel de Ville, in the southwest corner of the square, and first right down Place de la Taconnerie to the **Cathédrale St-Pierre** (Jun–Sep: daily 9am–7pm; Oct–May: Mon–Sat 10am–noon, 2–5pm, Sun 11am–12.30pm, 1.30–5pm). There has been a cathedral on this site since the 12th century, but the building you see today dates mainly from the 16th century – its austere interior reflects the style and philosophy of Calvinist times. It was here that Jean Calvin preached between 1536 and 1564. The view of the city and the surrounding Jura and Alps from the North Tower is worth the climb. Remains at the archaeological site (Jun–Sep: Tues–Sun 11am–5pm; Oct–May: Tues–Sat 2–5pm, Sun 10am–noon, 2–5pm) in the crypt, indicating the early importance of this Christian site, include a fine late 4th-century mosaic floor and a water tank for baptising new followers.

Stroll down the Rue Otto-Barblan, which faces the cathedral, and turn left up the Rue du Puits-St-Pierre

Left: the historic Place du Bourg-de-Four
Right: figure on the Place

(just to your right is the house where Henri Dunant first set up the Red Cross) to find the **Maison Tavel** (Tues–Sun 10am–5pm). This is a substantial residence dating from the 14th century, with exhibitions showing the development of the city, and life in a grand town house, through the centuries. Continue up this street and you will arrive at the Rue de l'Hôtel de Ville, and, naturally enough, the city's sombre **Hôtel de Ville (Town Hall)** – which is the administrative headquarters of Geneva's city council. The oldest part of the town hall dates from the 15th century. The building has witnessed numerous historic events, such as the first Geneva Convention (1864), after which the International Red Cross was established, and, in 1920, the first Assembly of the League of Nations (forerunner of the United Nations). For lunch, try the traditional Restaurant de l'Hôtel de Ville opposite the town hall. In good weather, its quiet corner terrace looking down the flag-bedecked street can be a surprisingly sunny spot.

Walk along the Grand Rue (the continuation of the Rue de l'Hôtel de Ville), noticing the elaborate shop signs hanging over some doorways. Turn right into Rue de la Pélisserie and right again into Rue Jean Calvin where you will find the **Barbier-Müller Museum** (daily 11am–5pm) on the corner. The museum features a fantastic collection of everyday and ritual artefacts from a myriad of traditional peoples from Africa, Southeast Asia and Oceania. The range of beautiful items takes in sculpture, carving, textiles and jewellery.

Continuing up Rue Jean Calvin, if you need a break from the cultural sights, take the Rue du Perron left down towards the **Place du Molard** with its lavish flower stalls. You will cross **Rue du Marché–Rue de la Croix d'Or–Rue de Rive** with their department stores and jewellery shops. The side lanes leading to the old town have many specialist shops and eateries. The Tour du Molard, at the lake end of the Place du Molard, once formed part of the fortified walls surrounding 14th-century Geneva.

The Finest Museum

Depending on your stamina you may still want to devote an hour or so to Geneva's most wonderful museum – the **Musée d'Art et d'Histoire** (Tues–Sun 10am–5pm). Take the Rue de la Fontaine to the right, along Rue de Rive, into Place du Bourg-de-Four. At the fountain take Chaudronniers to the left and then continue on to Rue Charles-Galland. To the right, you will see the grand building that houses the museum. The five floors fea-

Above: Maison Tavel. **Right:** at the Musée d'Art et d'Histoire. **Far Right:** the Jet d'Eau

ture the three main collections – archaeology, fine arts and applied arts.

The old town is an obvious choice for dinner, with its many cafés and restaurants, particularly around the Place du Bourg-de-Four, but if you happen to be down at the lakeside on a warm summer's evening you might try the Café du Centre, Place du Molard 5, which is famous for its seafood.

From the **Quai du Mont-Blanc** you get a good view of one of Geneva's best-known symbols – the **Jet d'Eau**. This fountain, which sends a jet of water 140m (460ft) high, is more than 100 years old. It was initially developed (and situated a little further downstream) as a pressure valve to help cope with the force of the Rhône's waters whenever the Coulouvrenière hydraulic station's energy was not being used by the workshops linked to it. Today the fountain has its own pumping station and is activated from March to early October, though for obvious reasons it is shut down on windy days.

The Quai du Mont-Blanc is the starting point for a number of **lake cruises**. These vary in length and focus. The short cruise views some of the famous residences on the shore while a number of the longer trips include lunch or dinner. The Compagnie Générale de Navigation (CGN – get information and tickets on the Quai du Mont-Blanc), which operates the cruises, has among its fleet a number of 19th-century paddle steamers that evoke a more elegant age. The quay is also the port for the regular ferry services operating between the major towns and villages around the lake between April and October (there is a much reduced winter service).

Founder of the League of Nations

Walking up the Quai du Mont-Blanc and Quai Wilson you get a fine view of the lake and, on the left, the **Palais Wilson**. The palace was originally built in 1875 as a luxury hotel, then for a while after 1920 it served as the headquarters of the League of Nations (the building was named after Woodrow Wilson, American president 1913–21 and founder of the league). In the 1980s it was devastated by fire, but has since been completely renovated and is now the office of the UN High Commissioner for Human Rights.

Continue along the lake-front gardens; at the lovely but expensive Perle du Lac restaurant you will need to take a left to the Rue de Lausanne and then

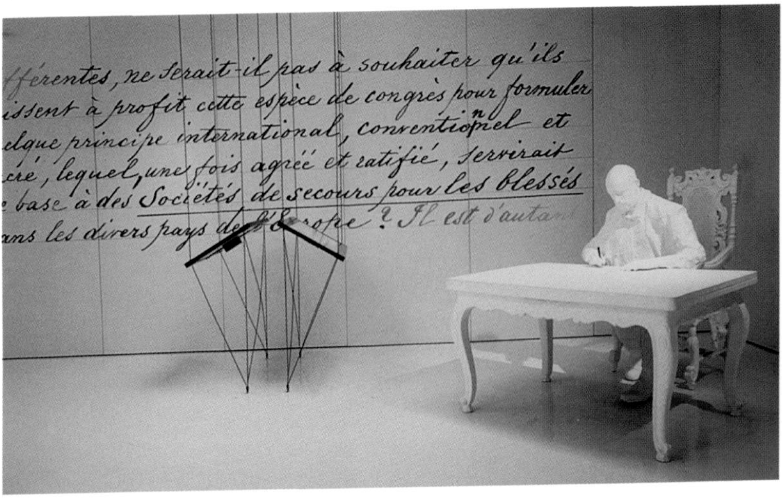

go right a little way along this road to get to the **Botanic Gardens** (Apr–Sep: daily 8am–7.30pm; Oct–Mar: 9.30am–5pm). These beautiful gardens were established in 1817 by the botanist A.P. de Candolle and its first glasshouse was constructed in 1908. The gardens have continued to develop over the years – recently a 'garden of the senses' has been created at the far end – and today they are an important centre for research in the botanical world. The 10,000 sq m (108,000 sq ft) of rockeries near the main entrance form one of the gardens' key displays. For the Genevoise, many of whom live in apartments, the gardens are a popular weekend recreation area, which on clear days affords the added attraction of good views of the Alps. In the centre of the gardens there's a small café. Leave by the gate on the Avenue de la Paix.

International Geneva

Continuing up and round the Avenue de la Paix, past the Place des Nations, you arrive at the **Palais des Nations**. This area is the heart of international Geneva – the offices of organisations such as the World Health Organisation, the UN High Commissioner for Refugees and the International Red Cross are all nearby. The Palais des Nations, a mixture of old and new buildings, set in splendid parkland, is the European headquarters of the United Nations. There is plenty to see here including the Museum of the League of Nations and the grand, frescoed Council Room – historically the scene of some of the most significant world political conferences. You might want to join one of the frequent tours of the Palais des Nations (Apr–Oct: daily 10am–noon, 2–4pm; Jul–Aug: daily 10am–5pm; Nov–Mar: Mon–Fri 10am–noon, 2–4pm).

If you decide to continue your tour in the international part of the city there are a couple of nearby museums worth visiting. On Avenue de la Paix,

opposite the entrance to the Palais des Nations, you will see the **Museum of the Red Cross and Red Crescent** (Wed–Mon 10am–5pm). This impressive museum is both an uplifting experience and a depressing catalogue of the work this humanitarian organisation undertakes to relieve the suffering caused by wars, famines and natural disasters. Dostoevsky's words (in French), which appear at the museum's entrance, reflect the approach and aim of the exhibition: 'Each of us is responsible for all that we see before us.' Back down the road from the Palais des Nations, a beautiful Neo-Renaissance mansion houses the **Musée Ariana** (Wed–Mon 10am–5pm). This museum's opulent collection of European, Middle Eastern and Asian ceramics and glass items, numbering more than 16,000 pieces, traces the development of this art form since the 9th century.

For dinner you could try Les Armures, Rue du Puits-St-Pierre 1, back in the heart of the old town. This traditional restaurant has lots of atmosphere, is cosy in winter and has a cool terrace for al fresco dining in the summer.

Excursion to Carouge

For a lighter day or half day away from the central sights and shops, Carouge – a southern suburb – makes for a delightful and easy trip. Take a tram (No 12 from Molard, or No 13 from Gare Cornavin). Carouge owes its character to King Victor Amadeus, Duke of Savoy and King of Sardinia. It was he who, in 1754, when the land was granted to the Kingdom of Sardinia, planned to build a city to rival powerful neighbour, Geneva. This aspiration was never realised, of course, but Carouge developed as an artisanal district. The pretty low-rise housing and shops in streets radiating off the tree-lined Place du Marché have several quaint features – wooden balconies and flower-filled courtyards – and the area has a distinct air of the Mediterranean.

Today the numerous cafés and bistros, antique and bric-à-brac shops still cater to a very local clientele and are a pleasantly low-key but rewarding attraction for visitors. It's a good idea to coincide your trip with the twice-weekly market that takes place in the **Place du Marché** on Wednesday and Saturday. The colourful produce stalls are a great place to pick up picnic fare.

The small **Museum of Carouge** (Tues–Sun 2–6pm during temporary exhibitions) is at Place de Sardaigne 2, behind the church in the Place du Marché. There are plenty of good restaurants in Carouge, which is a great location for dinner on a summer evening. A popular option is A l'Olivier de Provence at Rue Jacques-Dalphin 13, which serves classic Provençale food

Above Left: in the Red Cross Museum
Left: reclining on the Palais des Nations
Right: Place du Marché, Carouge

2. Lake Geneva *(see map, p27)*

The towns and countryside lining the northern side of Lake Geneva contain a pleasing mix of major sights, such as Château de Chillon, and quiet rural villages and lakeside towns. The narrow lakeside plain quickly gives rise to the foothills of the Jura. These south-facing slopes are covered in vines – wine is one of this region's major products. There are fine views of Mont-Blanc and the Alps on the other side of the lake.

Train links along this arc of countryside are good; the region can be explored in a day or two whether you travel by train or car. The Compagnie Générale de Navigation offers tours and ferry services which allow you to visit key lake-side places from Geneva, Lausanne and Montreux.

The oldest part of the small town of **Nyon** is located on a cliff overlooking the lake. The picturesque streets and squares of this ancient settlement (which was founded by the Romans in 45BC and known as Noviodunum), the tree-lined lakeside promenade, and the cultivated slopes in-between make this a pleasant venue for a half-day tour. The **Roman Museum** (Apr–Oct: Tues–Sun 10am–noon, 2–6pm; Nov–Mar: Tues–Sun 2–6pm) on Rue Maupertuis, off the Place du Château, is small but filled with interesting exhibits on aspects of everyday life, religion and the history of the Roman occupation of this part of Switzerland. There are some wonderful artefacts, many found locally, including beautifully decorated buckles and fine pots and glass for domestic use. Recent construction work uncovered the remains of an amphitheatre on Rue de la Porcelaine, which is now being excavated. The château is undergoing major refurbishment and is currently closed.

The lakeside is lined with plane trees and, at its western end, the **Musée du Léman** (Apr–Oct: Tues–Sun 10am–noon, 2–6pm; Nov–Mar: Tues–Sun 2–6pm), which focuses on the natural and cultural heritage of Lake Geneva (Lac Léman). The eastern end opens out and is home to a number of cafés. Here you will find the ferry stop for the boats that travel up and down the lake. You could take a short trip, across the lake, to Yvoire – a French village bursting with balconies and window boxes that overflow with geraniums in summer. Although Yvoire is something of a tourist honey pot, on a quiet weekday in summer it is an ideal destination for a short boat trip and lunch.

Prangins is a tiny village 2km (1¼ miles) to the east of Nyon. It is possible to walk there, or take the bus that departs hourly from outside Nyon station at the top end of the town. The striking Château de Prangins has recently been converted into a branch of the **Swiss National Museum** (Tues–Sun 10am–5pm). The house was built in the 1730s by a rich banker, Louis Guiguer, and has served both as a private house and a boys' boarding school. The museum's exhibits concentrate on Swiss life in the 18th and 19th centuries and, although it does not constitute the fullest of museum collections, the building and its grounds (check out the 18th-century walled garden planted in period style) are well worth the trip. There's a good café on one of the château's terraces.

Left: outside the Roman Museum, Nyon
Above Right: a paddle steamer on the lake

To Lausanne

If you have more than a day to explore the Lake Geneva area, **Lausanne** is definitely worth a visit. The city's attractions range from a medieval old town, with good shopping, to the Olympic Museum in the lake-shore district of Ouchy. The city is built on hills, so it can be tiring to explore, but there is a rail link between Ouchy and the old town.

Lausanne became the headquarters of the International Olympic Committee in 1915. The **Musée Olympique** (Tues–Sun 9am–6pm, Thur till 8pm) on the lake at the Quai d'Ouchy has an abundance of detailed information about the Olympic movement in particular and sports generally. The interactive exhibits and video footage should keep sports fans entertained for hours. Ouchy, with its lakeside esplanades, port and tempting cafés, is a relaxing place for a stroll.

The **old town** is situated on a rocky outcrop above Ouchy and the modern city. The cathedral, standing above the old town's squares and winding streets, is a great example of Gothic architecture. It was completed in 1275 and contains a number of treasures such as the rose window in the south transept. Views from the tower are spectacular. Between 10pm and 2am the night watch is still called out from the belltower – a tradition that has all but died out in the rest of Europe. The old town below the cathedral is a

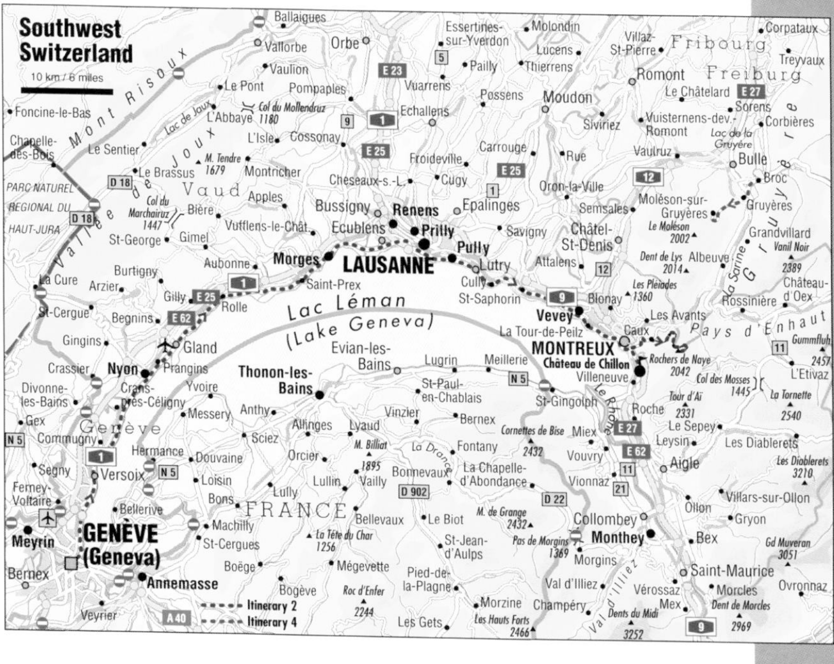

maze of winding streets filled with shops, restaurants and bars. The Place de la Palud and the Place de la Riponne have an excellent produce market with great bread, cheese and mushroom stalls as well as fruit and vegetables, on Saturday and Wednesday mornings. The city's fine town hall stands in the Place de la Palud. The Palais de Rumine in the Place de la Riponne houses a series of museums including the **Musée Cantonal des Beaux-Arts** (Tues–Wed 11am–6pm, Thur 11am–8pm, Fri–Sun 11am–5pm), and the **Musée Cantonal de Zoologie** (Tues–Thur 11am–6pm, Fri–Sun 11am–5pm), which has an interesting exhibition on mythical creatures such as the Loch Ness monster and the yeti.

The Swiss Riviera

Between Lausanne and Montreux the lake's shore is often known as the Swiss Riviera. The sunny climate, vine-clad hills, palm-lined lakeside walks, and marinas filled with expensive yachts are indeed redolent of the French Riviera – if you forget you can see the lake's far side. If you're driving to Montreux, follow the Lavaux wine route from Lausanne to Montreux via Lutry, Villette, Epesses, Dezaly, St Saphorin, Chardonne and Vevey. You will see a number of vineyards *(caveau)* whose proprietors welcome visitors for wine tasting.

Montreux grew as a resort in the late 19th century and today it is a major tourist and convention centre. It has a number of grand lakeside hotels built and furnished in belle époque style, the most notable of which are the Montreux Palace at Grand-Rue 100, and Eden du Lac at Rue du Théâtre 11.

The town's benign climate and dramatic location has long attracted celebrated residents and visitors. Among them were Ernest Hemingway, who visited Montreux in the 1920s; Noel Coward, who lived at Les Avants above the town in the 1960s; Vladimir Nabokov, who set up home in the Montreux Palace in the 1970s for the last years of his life; and the South African politician and statesman Paul Kruger. After the Boer War in 1902 Kruger retired to the Quartier des Villas Dubochet, an unusual development of serviced villas on the lakeside at Clarens between Montreux and Vevey. Along the lake shore, the glorious gardens are well tended – this is the **Chemin Fleuri**, which stretches for several kilometres from west of Montreux to Chillon east of the town – and make for delightful strolls, especially in spring when the rhododendrons and azaleas are in full bloom.

Montreux's number one attraction actually lies 2km (1¼ miles) to the east along the lake. **Château de Chillon** (Apr–Sep: daily 9am–6pm; Mar and Oct: 9.30am–5pm; Nov–Feb: 10am–4pm) was constructed in the 11th century as a fortress and was later extended to become a royal residence for the

Above: buy fresh mushrooms at the produce markets in the old town

dukes of Savoy. It occupies a striking strategic location on a rocky outcrop on the important medieval route between France and Italy via the St Bernard Pass. In 1536 it was taken by Bernese forces as part of Bern's conquest of the lakeside region and remained under the city's control until 1798. The castle has a number of literary associations, most notably with Lord Byron, who in 1816 wrote *The Prisoner of Chillon* about the imprisonment of the reformer François de Bonivard in the 1530s. The novelists Victor Hugo and Alexandre Dumas, and the painter J. M. W. Turner, were also inspired by this historic location. The red-roofed castle jutting out on a promontory in the lake is one of the best-known images of Switzerland.

Hiking Opportunities

For spectacular views of the lake, the Jura, and the Alps beyond, the cogwheel train journey up to **Rochers de Naye** (2,042m/6,700ft) is a good half-day excursion. The train leaves from the main station at Montreux for an hour-long journey with a couple of pretty stops on the way. There are restaurants at the top and at the stops of Glion and Caux. You can walk stretches of the route, and the trails at the top provide more hiking opportunities. The route west over the high slopes to Les Pléiades takes around six hours; you can get a train from there to Vevey and back to Montreux.

Montreux has an excellent music scene – the prestigious Montreux Jazz Festival is staged here in July. And in late August and September there's a festival of classical music.

Above: Château de Chillon
Right: model ferry on Lake Geneva

3. Watch-Making Towns of the Jura *(see map, p31)*

Neuchâtel and La Chaux-de-Fonds are two of the largest towns in northwest Switzerland. The former, which is the regional capital and an ancient religious and university town, lies on the shore of Lake Neuchâtel. La Chaux-de-Fonds, situated up in the foothills of the Jura, is known as a major centre of Swiss watch-making.

These towns are a couple of hours' drive from Geneva, or just over an hour from Bern. Both are easily accessible by train, but a car allows you to take some of the minor routes along the Jura and is useful if you are planning to do some walking or cross-country skiing in the Jura – which is particularly well equipped for these outdoor pursuits. There are hourly trains between the two towns and you will be able to visit both places in a full day.

The ancient university town of **Neuchâtel** has a number of interesting sights and an attractive location on the shores of Switzerland's largest lake. Along the front the quays are lined with gardens and there are cruises and ferries that take in some of the small vineyard villages to the west of Neuchâtel. Smaller than the Valais, the vineyards of this region produce a number of good Swiss wines including Perdrix Blanche. Walking up from the lake towards the old town, the Café du Théâtre, at Faubourg du Lac 1, is a nicely faded bar in which to have a coffee. Carrying on into the **old town** look out for the Wodey-Suchard sign and tea room along Rue Seyron. This is where, in 1825, Philippe Suchard made his first chocolate and opened a shop.

The Place des Halles, the town's ancient market square, is lined with solid 17th-century buildings. One of the oldest is the wonderfully picturesque **Maison des Halles**. This turreted, finely carved edifice was built in 1569 for the Orléans-Longueville family who ruled the area until the 18th century. Today it is a restaurant. The streets of the old town radiating off the Places de Halles, including the Rue des Moulins, are pleasant places for a stroll.

Walk up to the **Collegiate Church and Château** (guided tours Apr–Sep: Mon–Fri 10am–1pm, 2–5pm, Sat 10am–noon, 2–5pm, Sun 2–5pm) via Escalier du Château and Rue du Château. These partly Romanesque buildings command excellent views of the city. The church's fascinating features include the beautifully sculpted medieval cenotaph of the counts of Neuchâtel. A statue of Guillaume Farel, Neuchâtel's 16th-century reformer, stands in front of the entrance. The castle, once the seat of the ruling family, is mainly 15th- and 16th-century and today is home to the local cantonal government.

Just below the castle you will find the **Tour des Prisons** (Apr–Sep: daily 8am–6pm), which is the city's oldest building. Here there are models of the city in the Middle Ages and also great views of the city and across to the Alps.

Try the Maison des Halles, back down in the Places des Halles, for lunch. Choose between a café menu

Left: La Villa Schwob (1915) at La Chaux-de-Fonds, by Le Corbusier

on the ground floor and the more elevated fare of the renowned restaurant on the first floor.

While in Neuchâtel you might want to see a number of other attractions. Foremost of these is the **Musée d'Art et d'Histoire** (Tues–Sun 10am–5pm) along Esplanade Léopold-Robert on the lake front, which houses Swiss and Impressionist paintings and pieces representing the city's watch-making tradition. Of these exhibits, look out for some wonderful 18th-century clockwork figures – the Writer, the Musician and the Draughtsman, created by Jacquet-Droz.

A Watch-making Tradition

La Chaux-de-Fonds is the largest of the watch-making towns of the Jura (which includes Le Locle and Travers). Watch-making became established in Switzerland during the Reformation when Calvin persuaded goldsmiths to stop making elaborate religious items. The industry became concentrated in the towns of the Jura, and today it employs tens of thousands and contributes greatly to Switzerland's export income.

La Chaux-de-Fonds, unlike most Swiss cities, is built on a rigid grid pattern, following a fire at the end of the 18th century that destroyed much of the town. The car designer Louis Chevrolet and the architect Charles Edouard Le Corbusier are both sons of La Chaux-de-Fonds. Although Le Corbusier moved away from the city as a young man there are places in the city that are associated with him, including the house where he was born and the high school that he attended. You can get a Le Corbusier itinerary from the tourist information office (Espacité 1).

The **Musée International d'Horlogerie** (Jun–Sep: Tues–Sun 10am–6pm; Oct–May: Tues–Sun 10am–noon, 2–5pm) on the Rue des Musées is central and well worth a visit. The museum has thousands of watches, time-pieces and automata and presents man's exploration and measurement of time. Among the highlights is a collection of 17th-century enamel watches. Antique clocks and watches are restored in a workshop, which is on view to the public.

Above: detail, the Collegiate Church, Neuchâtel

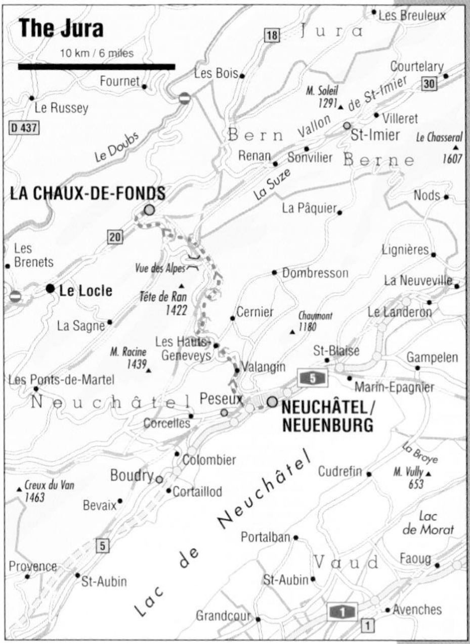

4. Gruyères *(see map, p27)*

Gruyères is one of the country's best-preserved medieval towns. It is a hilltop fortress, complete with château, cobbled market street and sweeping views to the surrounding alpine pastures. At Moléson-sur-Gruyères you can see traditional production of the cheese that takes the town's name, and at Broc you can visit a Nestlé chocolate factory.

Gruyères is high on the list of tour bus destinations; Gruyères and Broc both have train stations if you're not driving. Gruyères is pedestrianised so all vehicles must be left at a car park just below the town. It's a compact town so you don't have to walk far to see all the attractions. It is also a hugely popular resort so visit outside the main summer season or early or late in the day if you want to avoid the crowds. You can take in Gruyères and either Moléson-sur-Gruyères or Broc in a day.

The town of **Gruyères** has grown little since medieval times, partly because of its restricted hilltop position. It consists of little more than a main street that leads up to a splendid château. Once through the gateway the main street widens out – originally this was to provide a space for markets and fairs. Many of the facades have retained their medieval appearance and some of the buildings, especially at the end near the château, feature beautiful stone and woodwork exhibited by Gothic tracery and Renaissance detailing. Notice also the signs and emblems displaying a crane (*grue* in French) after which the town is named.

13th-Century Dungeons

The **Château de Gruyères** (Apr–Oct: 9am–6pm; Nov–Mar: 10am–4.30pm) dates mainly from the 15th century – the original building was destroyed by fire. Only the dungeons remain of the 13th-century castle. Treasures in the beautifully decorated and furnished rooms include fine Flemish tapestries and 19th-century murals depicting the exploits of the counts of Gruyères, who ruled from the 11th to the 16th century. In the mid-16th century the château was owned by the city states of Fribourg and Bern, whose bailiffs took up residence. From 1848 till 1938 it was privately owned before again becoming Fribourg state property.

Within the château there is the rather unexpected **Museum H.R. Giger**

Above: Gruyères. **Right:** cheese-making
Far Right: Château de Gruyères

(Apr–Oct: Tues–Sun 10am–6pm; Nov–Mar: Tues–Fri 11am–5pm, Sat–Sun 10am–6pm). This museum exhibits paintings, sketches and models by the Swiss surrealist H.R. Giger. If his work looks familiar you have probably seen the film *Alien*, for which Giger was the award-winning designer.

The people of Gruyères pride themselves on keeping various rural crafts alive. Among the welter of tourist trinkets that are available in the town you are likely to find some excellent original woodcarving, pottery items, and, of course, local delicacies such as cheese and chocolate. There are plenty of places for lunch here but you could not do better than try the Café-Restaurant Les Remparts on the left as you walk up towards the château. Be sure to sample a *raclette* or fondue, or some other dish incorporating Gruyères's most famous product.

You won't have missed the fact that the famous Gruyères cheese is made locally and there are a couple of places where you can see it being manufactured. Pringy, beside the Gruyères railway station, is one such dairy, but if you have a car, or if you fancy the two-hour walk (along Via les Reybes) it is better to go to Moléson-sur-Gruyères. This is a small resort southwest of Gruyères where there is a 17th-century alpine cheese dairy (mid-May–mid-Oct: daily 9.30am–7pm). Here cheese is made according to traditional methods – the milk is heated in an enormous cauldron over an open fire. Cheese-making demonstrations take place at 10am and 3pm. The dairy has a restaurant and a small shop.

Chocolate Heaven

The small town of **Broc** a few kilometres northeast of Gruyères has a Nestlé factory famous for making the delicious Cailler range of chocolates. The **Broc Nestlé Factory** (Mar–Oct: Mon–Fri 9–11am, 1.30–4pm; closed for two to three weeks in July) was established at the end of the 19th century by the grandson of François Louis Cailler, who was the first person to mechanise the production of Swiss chocolate, in Vevey in 1819. Unfortunately, for hygiene reasons, it is no longer possible to visit the factory floor; the guided tour comprises a film presentation, an opportunity to sample the products, and a visit to the shop.

5. The Valais *(see map below)*

The western end of the Valais (Rhône Valley) is a delightful, dramatic region in which to spend two or three days. The resort of Verbier buzzes in the season. In summer, when the local trails attract hikers, it's quieter. The ancient towns of Sion and Sierre are full of history, and Zermatt at the foot of the Matterhorn – a mecca for skiers and mountaineers alike – is *the* vantage point from which to see the country. Sion and Sierre both make ideal bases for a few days' exploration of the Valais.

Travelling by car allows you to see the sights of the Valais easily but all the towns are accessible by public transport. Sion and Sierre, in the bottom of the valley, are served by mainline stations, both well located for the centre of town. Le Châble is the station for Verbier, from which a bus or cable car (in winter) travels up to the resort. Zermatt is car-free – vehicles can be parked at Täsch, the last stop before Zermatt on the line from Brig or Visp.

The large resort of **Verbier** was nothing more than a small hamlet 50 years ago when a ski lift to the peak of Les Ruinettes was inaugurated. Since then, cable cars and lifts have facilitated the development of numerous slopes. In 1999 two old chair lifts at Lac des Vaux were replaced, almost doubling capacity to 2,400 people an hour. From 50,000 passengers in 1950, Verbier's ski lifts now register more than 12 million a year.

The **Mont-Fort** glacier above the resort has all-year skiing and snowboarding. With 400km (250 miles) of ski runs and 95 lifts, the resort offers something for all levels of skiers and is popular with both Swiss weekenders and foreigners. The Patrouille des Glaciers, one of Verbier's most famous events (dating to World War II, when Swiss alpine soldiers trained on the 54km [33-mile] Verbier–Zermatt route) is held in even years in early May.

In summer the resort is a fine location for hiking or mountain biking – there

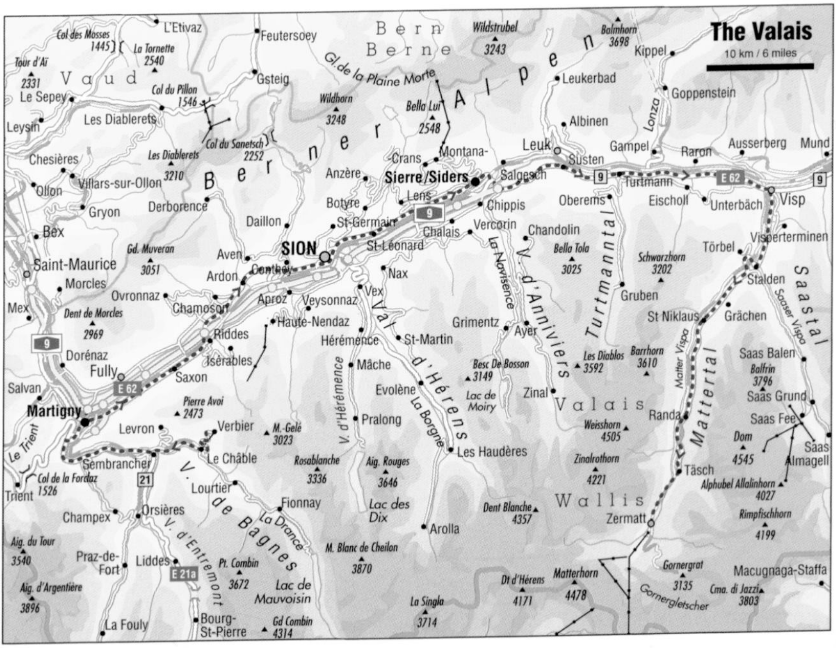

are 400km (250 miles) of marked paths that link peaks, viewpoints and Val de Bagnes villages. For a mix of culture and outdoor activities plan your trip for late July/early August to coincide with the Verbier Music Festival, featuring an eclectic programme of music with the accent on the classical.

Place Centrale is the heart of town and has, shops, restaurants, a post office and a tourist information office (Mon–Fri 8am–noon, 2–6.30pm, Sat 9am–noon, 4–6.30pm, Sun 9am–noon; open later Dec–Apr) with details on accommodation, sporting facilities, lessons, hiking routes and events. There are ample options for lunch in and around the centre of the village, but for a traditional Valaisan experience try Chez Dany (closed May and Nov), half an hour's walk from Les Ruinettes cable car station. You can tell that après-ski is taken seriously in Verbier from the huge number of bars and eateries.

Hiking Networks

There is an ample choice of hikes from Verbier in the Val de Bagnes and you are bound to find one to suit you: long or short, high or low altitude, strenuous or easy. Ask at the tourist office for information on the different routes. There are mountain restaurants and cable cars open throughout the summer but be warned that the weather can change quite quickly.

One easy half-day circular route starts from Les Ruinettes (the cable car station above Verbier reached from Télécabine de Médran). The first 1½-hour stretch, to Cabane Mont-Fort, follows the route of a *bisse* – a traditional irrigation channel.

Cabane Mont-Fort is an old mountain refuge with a delightful restaurant. The journey back via La Chaux takes just over an hour. There are great views on this walk to the surrounding peaks. Listen for the high pitched whistling of marmots along the route, especially at the highest points. If you want to make a whole day of it there are several routes down to Verbier from Les Ruinettes – taking from three to four hours.

Other lower level routes from Verbier include one to Le Châble (and on to Bruson), and to Sarreyer and Fionnay. These Valais villages retain much more of their original rustic charm than the higher settlements that have become ski resorts. There is a well developed and varied walking-route network throughout the Val de Bagnes, with both high mountain routes and lower valley trails. When planning your trip, bear in mind that Sion and Sierre are well situated bases for getting to all locations in the Valais on an extended stay.

Above: the Val de Bagnes is great for hiking
Right: a statue honours the local marmot population

Roman Foundations

Martigny, originating in Roman times and situated in the bend of the Rhône where the river starts to head north towards Lake Geneva, offers a good break from the activity-based recreation of Verbier. Today the southwest part of the town, around the **Rue du Bourg**, is the most interesting. Two major sights are the recently excavated Roman amphitheatre, just south of the centre and, nearby, the Fondation Pierre Gianadda.

The **amphitheatre** is used for special events such as the annual Combat de Reines (cow fights) in October. The contestants are rarely injured in this event, which is the culmination of a series of fights still staged in the villages of the Valais throughout the summer. Continued today for reasons of tradition and tourism, these fights once determined which cow would lead the herd up to the high alpine pastures for summer grazing.

The diverse attractions at the **Fondation Pierre Gianadda** (Jun–Nov: 9am–7pm; Dec–May: 10am–6pm) include a Gallo-Roman museum displaying archaeological finds from the area, a fine collection of classic cars and a growing collection of fine art with works by Modigliani, Cézanne and Goya.

Perched Sion

The dramatic configuration of **Sion**, the capital of the Valais, is obvious from the motorway. Perched atop the two craggy pinnacles that dominate the town are the Church of Notre-Dame de Valère and the ruins of the castle of Tourbillon. Both can be reached by short steep climbs from the top end of the Rue des Châteaux. The **Church of Notre-Dame de Valère** (Jun–Sep: Mon–Sat 10am–6pm, Sun 2–6pm; Oct–May: Tues–Sat 10am–5pm,

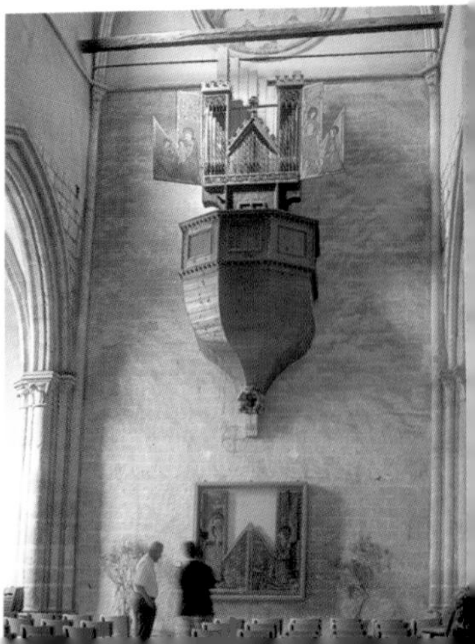

Above: the way to the Church of Notre-Dame de Valère, Sion. **Right:** the church's interior

Sun 2–5pm) was built in the 12th century by the bishops of Sion who, for almost 800 years until 1848, controlled much of the Valais. Highlights in the church include intricately carved stalls and a 15th-century organ (reputedly the world's oldest playable organ). The ruined exterior walls of **Tourbillon** (mid-Mar–mid-Nov: Tues–Sun 10am–6pm) are all that remain of the once glorious summer palace of the bishops of Sion. From both the Valère and Tourbillon peaks, the views of the rooftops of Sion and the Valais beyond are impressive.

Head down into town, where there are a number of interesting buildings to explore. Take Rue des Châteaux, and you will pass the Au Vieux Valais restaurant, Rue St Théodule 3, which serves traditional fare and makes a good stop for lunch. The **Hôtel de Ville** (take the tourist office tour to see this), with its sumptuous first-floor council chamber, is at the end of the street. Cross over Rue du Grand-Pont to the **Cathédrale Notre-Dame du Glarier** with its Romanesque belfry. The **Sorcerers' Tower** (Jun–Sep: Tues–Sun 1–6pm; Oct– May: Tues–Sun 1–5pm) on Avenue Ritz is a remnant of the city's medieval walls. The **Maison Supersaxo** (Mon–Fri 8am–noon, 2–6pm), tucked away just off Rue de Lausanne, is a Gothic mansion dating to 1505. Check out its staircase and second-floor ceiling rose in particular.

Sunny Sierre

Though it was greatly expanded in the 20th century, the valley town of **Sierre** remains attractive; its boast of being the sunniest town in Switzerland adds to its appeal and to the quality of wines produced in the area. The **Rue du Bourg** is the town's old main street. Here you will find down-at-heel antique shops and well-stocked cafés, both of which are quite inviting to those in search of ways to fill a lazy half hour. You will also find the pretty **Hôtel de Ville** (Mon–Fri 9–11am, 3–5pm), whose fine interior decoration, consisting of frescoes and stained glass, makes it well worth a visit.

Also worth seeing is the Château de Villa, above the town. This lovely old building houses the **Musée Valaisan de la Vigne et du Vin** (Mar–Oct: Tues–Sun 2–5pm; Nov–Dec: Fri–Sun 2–5pm, Jan–Feb: on demand), which has a small exhibition, a tasting centre and bar. Here you can taste and buy all the wines of the Valais, Switzerland's premier producing region. There is also a delightful restaurant with a large terrace. The museum is the starting point for a 6.5-km (4-mile) marked trail through the vineyards to **Salgesch**, a small vineyard village east of Sierre. The walk there and back is probably best attempted before tasting sessions and lunch. Sierre has none of the glitz of the bigger towns and resorts but makes a fine base for exploring the valley and has good bars and restaurants in which to relax after the day's exertions.

Above: the Church of Notre-Dame de Valère as seen from Tourbillon

Under the Matterhorn

Zermatt, with its wonderful location at the foot of the 4,478-m (14,688-ft) high **Matterhorn**, is a classic alpine resort. In 1865, with the aid of two Swiss guides, British illustrator, Edward Whymper, became the first person to succeed in reaching the peak. (Tragically, his fellow climbers died on the descent.) Thereafter Zermatt became a mountaineering and skiing centre. The enterprising Seiler family who ran the **Monte Rosa Hotel**, where early mountaineers stayed, is still a famous name among hoteliers and has developed a chain of establishments to cater for the growing number of visitors. Today the resort is a fabulous centre that offers all-year-round skiing – the highest in the country – incomparable views, and great hiking in summer (guides and organised tours are available from the tourist office in Bahnhofplatz).

The oldest part of Zermatt, **Hinterdorf**, up to the left of the main street, is packed with traditional Valais chalets and *mazots* (barns). The parish church on the main square and the cemetery are worth visiting – you will find tombstones of mountaineers for whom the slopes of the Matterhorn were the last they scaled. To the left of the main street is the **Alpine Museum** (Jun–Oct: 10am–noon, 4–6pm; Dec–Apr: Sun–Fri 4.30–6.30pm) which provides a history of the development of Zermatt, and exhibits on the early mountaineers and the Matterhorn. Behind the Alpine Museum, the presence of a small English church is an indication of the lure Zermatt has had for English visitors and mountaineers for the past 150 years.

Trains and Cable Cars

For a fabulous view of the Matterhorn and the surrounding peaks and glaciers, take the rack railway up to Gornergrat. A cable car will take you on up to Stockhorn at 3,532m (11,585ft), but the highest accessible point is the cable car station on Klein Matterhorn, which also provides superb views. The Glacier Express train service between Zermatt and St Moritz is an eight-hour journey through spectacular scenery, and a particularly memorable, if expensive way to reach or leave Zermatt.

Central Switzerland

6. Bern *(see map, p40)*

A day spent exploring the impressive old town of Switzerland's capital, Bern, on foot, taking in a varied selection of fine, historic architecture, interesting museums, an abundance of fountains, and enough shops, tea rooms and restaurants to tempt every taste.

The beautifully preserved old town of Bern is situated on a low hill overlooking a loop of the Aare River. It is compact – less than 2km (1¼ miles) long – and the arcaded main streets make exploring a joy whatever the weather. Its main sights can be covered in a day. Riverside parks and gardens and a number of historic platz *(squares) provide areas in which to sit and watch the world go by.*

The city of **Bern** was founded by the Duke of Zähringen at the end of the 12th century and had close ties with Burgundy. The 13th century was a period of considerable growth and autonomy. The city became independent of Burgundy and in 1353 it joined the Swiss Confederation. As the inhabitants' wealth and power increased – at one stage the lands around Lake Geneva came under Bernese influence – grander stone houses and public buildings were erected. It is these 16th- and 17th-century buildings that you see today. The invasion by Napoleon in 1798 saw the end of Bern's territorial ambitions, but in 1848 it was selected as the seat of the Swiss parliament. The old town, whose arcades, cobbled streets and graceful architecture have remained largely intact for more than 400 years, is now a World Heritage Site.

Start the tour at the **Bundesplatz**, not far from the main railway station. Here you can observe the colourful fresh-produce market that is held on Bundesplatz and Bärenplatz every morning in summer (in winter, Tuesday and Saturday only). Have a coffee at Gfeller on the Kochergasse side of Bärenplatz, as the shoppers and traders go about their business.

An Annual Transformation

If you happen to be here on the fourth Monday in November, be sure to check out an event that happens only once a year. This is the date when Bundesplatz and Bärenplatz and the centre of the old town are transformed by the Zibelemärit (Onion Market). Hundreds of stallholders set up shop and the city takes on a distinctly festive air.

Above Left: Edward Whymper. **Left:** the rack railway. **Right:** Bern's Bundeshaus

At the southern end of the square is the Swiss Parliament, or **Bundeshaus** (free 45-minute guided tours: Mon–Fri 9am–noon, 2–5pm). Its buildings date from between 1851 and 1902, although Bern has been the country's capital since 1848. Take the terrace walk via the right-hand side of the main building behind the Bundeshaus– which overlooks the river and suburbs to the mountains beyond – and head for the Kirchenfeldbrücke (bridge). Turn right and cross the bridge, with its views of the river and cathedral, carrying on into Helvetiaplatz. Straight ahead is the **Bernisches Historisches Museum** (Tues–Sun 10am–5pm, Wed till 8pm).

Thousand Flower Tapestry

This castle of a museum gives a good introduction to the city's history. Most notable among its wonderful, multifarious treasures is the Thousand Flower Tapestry, created in 1466 and acquired by Bern 10 years later as part of the Burgundian booty. There are lots of other attractions in this museum, including fine Meissen and other 18th-century porcelain, such as Franz Anton Bustelli's delicate harlequins dating from 1760. There is also a good exhibit on Niklaus Manuel's 1517 *Dance of Death* paintings. If you linger at the museum, its Bistro Steinhalle restaurant is a good lunch option.

Cross back over the bridge into the old town and you pass the Concert Hall Casino before turning right down Münstergasse. This brings you to one of Bern's most impressive landmarks, the late-Gothic **cathedral** (Easter–Oct: Tues–Sat 10am–5pm, Sun 11.30am–5pm; Nov–Easter: Tues–Fri 10am–noon, 2–4pm, Sat 10am–noon, 2–5pm, Sun 11.30am–2pm). Construction started

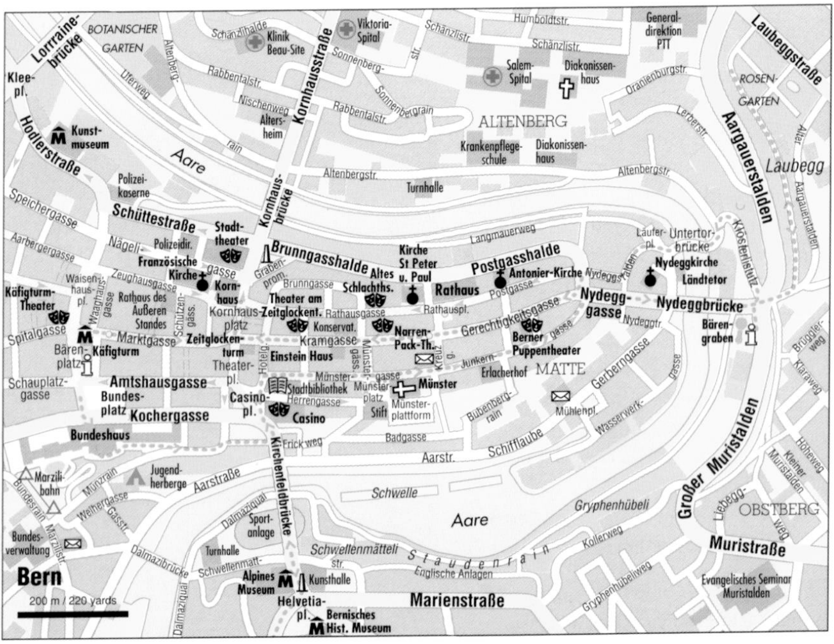

in 1421 under the direction of Matthäus Ensinger and took more than 100 years. The stained glass (see the *Dance of Death* window) and choir stalls, with their scenes of everyday Bernese life, are particularly noteworthy. The present spire, at 100m (328ft) the highest in Switzerland, was built in 1893. The beautifully painted and carved main portal of the *Last Judgement* is a masterpiece. One of Bern's many fountains stands in Münsterplatz; this, the Moses Fountain (1790), is a fine example. A good lunch option is Frohsinn (Münstergasse 54).

Turn right down Junkerngasse where you might like to stop and admire No 47, **Erlacherhof**. This stately baroque residence was built around 1750 for the then mayor, von Erlach. The house, its courtyard and gardens have been restored, and it is still the seat of the mayor of Bern. If you continue right down Junkerngasse (notice the beautiful frieze on No 22) and on across Nydeggbrücke you will see Bern's famous **Bear Pits** (Bärengraben) to the right (summer: 8am–5.30pm; winter: 9am–4pm). According to legend, the founder of Bern, Duke Berchtold V Zähringen, ordered the city to be named after the first animal killed in the forests that covered the lands where the city now stands. Today, as you will notice, the bear is the city's emblem. Originally in Bärenplatz, the pits were moved to the current site in 1857. They were made more bear-friendly, and in 1996 the bears' numbers were restricted to five. If you want to see bear cubs, Easter is the most likely time; cubs are usually born around January and start to make public appearances in the spring. For the best view of the old town in the meander of the Aare River take the path left up above Aargauerstalden to the **Rose Garden**.

Retracing your steps back down to the river, cross the Untertorbrücke, which is the city's oldest bridge, dating from 1461, then take Nydeggstalden into Gerechtigkeitsgasse. Halfway up you'll see the **Justice Fountain** which dates from 1543, and is the first of a series of medieval fountains that punctuate this route up through the old town. This symbolic representation has Justice surrounded by the Pope, Emperor, Mayor and Sultan.

Kramgasse

Continue on to **Kramgasse**. This is the heart of the arcaded old town and the fine 16th-century buildings are today occupied by an interesting variety of shops and restaurants.

No 49, **Einstein Haus** (Mar–Oct: Tues–Fri 10am–5pm, Sat 10am–4pm), which was the home of Albert Einstein from 1903–1905, displays copies of some of the great scientist's writings. Rizz (Kramgasse 57) sells cakes and pastries and has a small tea room if you're in need of afternoon refreshments.

Above left: the bear is Bern's emblem
Right: the much-loved clock tower

The **Zähringen Fountain**, which commemorates the city's founder, dates from 1535 and is situated towards the top end of Kramgasse. Kramgasse ends with the **Clock Tower** or **Zeitglockenturm**. Together with the emblem of the bear, and the cathedral, this is one of the city's most popular and enduring sights. The tower marks the official centre of Bern and used to inform the inhabitants of the precise time. The original tower bell was augmented, in 1530, by the remarkable and delightful astronomical clock and figure play, both the work of Kaspar Brunner. The figure play, an intricate mechanism involving a rooster, lion, jester, knight in armour and a procession of bears, plays out a series of movements just before and during the chiming of the hour. At one time this tower marked the western limit of the old town.

Beyond the Clock Tower you will find **Marktplatz**. Check out the quaint kiosks on the Marktplatz side of the clock tower. Marktplatz continues the run of arcaded streets and ends with the **prison tower** which dates from 1643 and was used as a prison until 1897. Just in front of the prison tower is the **Anna Seiler Fountain**. The original statue from this fountain (now displayed in the Bernisches Historisches Museum), dating from 1549, is an allegory of the noted Swiss trait of moderation. Return down Marktgasse and turn left down to the **Kornhaus** (Feb–Nov: Tues–Fri 10am–7pm, Sat–Sun 10am–5pm). This building, originally a grain market hall, dates from the early 18th century. It has been completely renovated and today it serves as a multimedia and design exhibition space. There is a lively bar in its cellar, which is a good place to unwind after your wanderings.

Authentic Cuisine

You certainly won't find a shortage of places to eat in the old town. If it's an authentic taste of the capital's cuisine that you're after, you should definitely sample the offerings at Harmonie (Hotelgasse 3, closed weekends). This restaurant, reputedly the oldest in the city, serves great traditional fare, such as fondue, sausages, and tripe.

If you want to use Bern as a base for some of the nearby itineraries – situated at the centre of the country's extensive rail network it's a good choice – a recommended place to stay is Adler Hotel (Gerechtigkeitsgasse 7, tel: 031-311 1725) which is in the heart of the old town and has a range of moderately priced rooms.

Above and Left: decorative touches on buildings in Bern. **Right:** the Hasle-Rüegsau bridge, Emmental

7. Emmental *(see map, p44)*

The Emmental region is characterised by the gently rolling hills of the Emme Valley. It is from these rich pastures that Emmental cheese is produced. The landscape is dotted with traditional barns and farmhouses, and rivers and streams forded by old wooden covered bridges. This tour passes through several interesting towns and villages.

This approx 80-km (50-mile) route is designed for a day's leisurely driving, with interesting stops en route. If you're based in Bern the motorway journey back from Thun should take just over half an hour.

Start at **Burgdorf**, 20km (12 miles) northeast of Bern. The 12th-century castle, once part of the dukes of Zähringen's land, is the town's leading landmark. Continuing south, take the main road to Hasle. It's worth getting out of the car here and walking to the old bridge, just west of the main settlement of **Hasle-Rüegsau** which spans both sides of the river. Dating from 1838, this is the largest covered wooden bridge in Europe.

Take the road north up to **Affoltern**, where you can see the region's cheese being made at the impressive Schaukäserie Emmental cheese dairy (daily 8.30am–6.30pm). Then head south on the main road via **Sumiswald** – a pretty little village with the characteristic overhanging arched gable much in evidence – to **Langnau im Emmental**, the region's small main town.

Continuing east a few kilometres will bring you to **Trubschachen**, another attractive Emmental village which produces pretty local pottery. Turn round and head back; just out of Trubschachen take the minor road left to **Aeschau,** where you should turn left towards **Eggiwil**. Then follow the scenic road south and west from Eggiwil through Siehen, Oberei and Schwarzenegg to Steffisburg and the larger town of **Thun**.

Thun is a major town with a medieval old quarter and a lakeside setting. Obere Hauptgasse, one of the prettiest streets, has first-floor terraces that act as footpaths above the arcaded shops. You'll find lots of lunch options around the Rathausplatz main square. If you have time, 2km (¼ mile) east along the lake, **Schloss Oberhofen** (mid-May–mid-Oct: Tues–Sun 11am–5pm, Mon 2–5pm) is a splendid 13th-century mansion with a highly impressive collection of antique furniture, and graceful gardens.

8. Bernese Oberland *(see map below)*

The Bernese Oberland at the northern edge of the Alps forms a classic Swiss landscape, with clear lakes and rolling hills to the north and the mighty peaks of the Eiger and Jungfrau in the south. Interlaken, the main resort, sits between the lakes of Thun and Brienz. Near Brienz, Ballenberg, the open-air museum, presents Switzerland's vernacular architecture and traditional arts and crafts on a large rural site.

It is easy to get a train to the villages in the Jungfrau region just south of Interlaken, from which you can hike through the gorgeous Swiss landscape. Ballenberg is also very accessible by public transport – taking the train to Brienz and then the special shuttle bus to the museum takes approximately 30 minutes from Interlaken. A couple of days will allow time to visit the Jungfrau region and Ballenberg.

Interlaken is first and foremost a tourist centre – virtually all short tours of the country will visit the town, with its classic lakeside setting and fantastic views of the Jungfrau and Eiger mountains; it is also a gateway to the pretty alpine valleys to the south in the Jungfrau region.

The old quarter of Unterseen in the northwest of the town, overlooking the Aare River, is particularly pretty. The main cobbled square here has a

number of attractive buildings including the **Museum of Tourism of the Jungfrau Region** (May–mid-Oct: Tues–Sun 2–5pm), which charts the development of tourism in this region of Switzerland.

From Wilderswil 2km (1¼ miles) south of Interlaken, you can take the cogwheel railway (Jun–Oct) up to Schynige Platte, which provides fantastic views of the peaks to the south, and which is the start of a number of hiking trails. There's also an alpine botanical garden here where you can see edelweiss and other native flora.

Jungfrau Region

The area to the south of Interlaken is one of pretty alpine valleys, waterfalls and small picturesque villages and resorts, presided over by the Jungfrau massif with its mighty peaks – Jungfrau (4,158m/13,638ft), Mönch (4,107m/13,474ft) and Eiger (3,970m/13,025ft). The Lauterbrunnen and Lütschental valleys are the main routes into this region. In winter it is a popular skiing destination and in summer it offers some of the best and most varied hiking in Switzerland. Transport (trains and cable cars) is extensive. It's not difficult to plan a day's hiking as the train journey from Interlaken to the heart of the region is quick and easy. The **Lauterbrunnen Valley** has the most dramatic scenery and lots of opportunities for outdoor activity, whatever the season.

The main small resorts of Mürren and Wengen are both picture-postcard villages and car-free. Both offer good skiing and excellent hiking. Take the walk from Mürren to the small village of Gimmelwald at the head of the valley, and from there you can take a cable car up to the 2,970m (9,745ft) Schilthorn peak with the famous revolving restaurant, Piz Gloria, that featured in the James Bond film, *On Her Majesty's Secret Service.*

The scenery in the **Lütschental Valley** is gentler than that of its westerly neighbour but again offers good skiing and hiking. Some of the trails around Grindelwald, the valley's large resort, stay open throughout the winter, so walking is possible all year round. The area above Grindelwald can be reached by cable car and from there you can branch out on any number of hiking trails in summer. Grindelwald spreads out over alpine pastures and offers an assortment of accommodation choices if you're planning a longer stay in the region.

Above: Unterseen square in Interlaken
Right: a classic lakeside setting

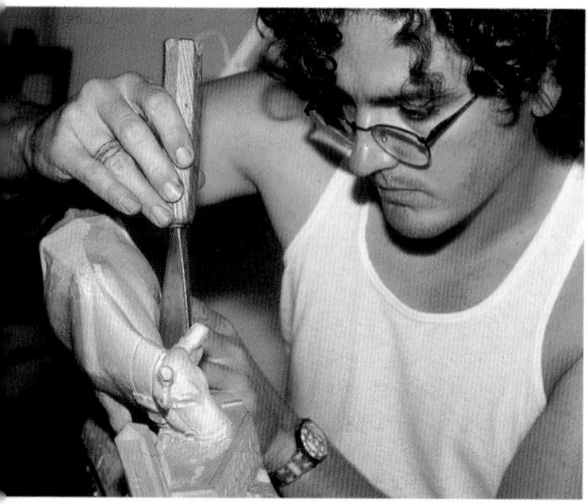

Ballenberg

The **Swiss Open-Air Museum Ballenberg** (mid-Apr–Oct: daily 9am–6pm, tel: 033-952 1030, www.ballenberg.ch) presents the country's rural architecture and culture in one bite-size piece. At 66 hectares (163 acres) it is a fairly large bite so give yourself a full day to take in the traditional buildings and some craft demonstrations. The museum, which opened over 20 years ago, has samples of vernacular architecture – real buildings moved piece by piece from all over the country. These are authentically furnished and some host craft demonstrations such as bread- and cheese-making, pottery, weaving, shingle-making and threshing. Some demonstrations are daily, others, such as threshing and resin-tapping, take place only every fortnight. At the shops around the museum site you can buy produce and craft items, and there are a number of delightful restaurants.

The vegetable plots and meadows that surround the buildings are tended in the traditional way, and you can see rare breeds of goat, sheep and hen. There are seasonal events such as Easter egg painting, alpine processions and harvest festivals and, for small groups, there are hands-on craft programmes.

9. Basel *(see map, p48)*

Basel, which straddles the Rhine and borders France and Germany, is an interesting mix of old and new. It has a fine old town with a splendid Renaissance town hall. There are also fascinating attractions that stem from its industrial heritage, and a range of museums.

The old town can be explored on foot in a couple of hours, leaving plenty of time for a leisurely lunch and an afternoon looking at a traditional paper mill and the house of a 19th-century ribbon manufacturer.

Basel is the country's second-largest city. Founded in Roman times, it was established at the last point where the Rhine is navigable to sea-going vessels, and is today a thriving modern port. During the Reformation it remained a tolerant city that welcomed French Huguenots, who introduced silk weaving. The city later became a centre for the manufacture of silk ribbon. The development of synthetic dyes to colour the ribbons made this the forerunner of the huge pharmaceuticals industry which today is one of the city's largest employers, with firms such as Novartis and Roche having headquarters here.

Start the day in **Marktplatz** which, from

Above: a wood carver in Ballenberg
Right: a portrait by Holbein at the Kuntsmuseum

early in the morning, is enlivened by its daily produce market. Don't miss the **Rathaus** (town hall), and the courtyard in particular. This early 16th-century building, still the seat of the canton's government, is painted a rich red and adorned with striking frescoes and tiles.

Take Marktgasse up to Fischmarkt and its replica Gothic fountain; the original 1390 fountain is in the Historisches Museum. Then go along Schneidergasse and on up Spalenberg – these streets are good for gifts and arts and crafts items. On reaching the top of Spalenberg turn left into Heuberg, with its medieval houses. Continue to the church and then wind your way down to the left into Barfüsserplatz. In the square the imposing Gothic church houses the **Historisches Museum** (Wed–Mon 10am–5pm). It has an interesting collection that displays the work of the medieval guilds, particularly goldsmiths. Try the Huguenin café (Barfüsserplatz 6) for a coffee break.

Statue of the Foolish Virgin

From the northern corner of the square, near the Huguenin café, follow Streitgasse and Münsterberg to the **Münster** (Easter–mid-Oct: Mon–Fri 10am–5pm, Sat 10am–4pm, Sun 1–5pm; mid-Oct–Easter: Mon–Sat 11am–4pm, Sun 2–4pm). See the 12th-century sandstone cathedral's imposing twin towers, the intricate friezes on the main door arches and interior, and the statue of the Foolish Virgin on the west facade. Turn right on Rittergasse, right into St Alban-Graben and you will reach one of the country's finest museums, the Kunstmuseum, on the corner.

The **Kunstmuseum** (Tues–Sun 10am–5pm) has an outstanding collection of 15th- and 16th-century Flemish paintings and is home to the world's largest collection of Holbeins. Notable works of Hans Holbein the Younger include *Portrait of the Artist's Wife with Her Children.* The museum also has an impressive range of 19th- and 20th-century art, with Cubism and Pop Art represented by Picasso, Mark Rothko and Andy Warhol. The work of a 19th-century Basel artist, Arnold Böcklin, is a less-known highlight.

For lunch you could try the city's oldest inn – Zum Goldenen Sternen

Above: Basel's town hall dates back to the early 16th century

(St Alban-Rheinweg 70), with ancient banqueting rooms and a terrace overlooking the river. Take St Alban-Vorstadt to the right up from the entrance of the Kunstmuseum and veer left down Mühlenberg; continue right once you reach the river and you will get to Zum Goldenen Sternen.

After lunch continue a little way along the river and you will come to the **Basler Papiermühle** (Tues–Sun 2–5pm). This beautiful old former paper and flour mill has been restored and is now a museum devoted to the history of paper-making and printing. The museum is interactive – you can make your own paper and print on it.

Go back up the hill via St Alban-Tal and turn right into St Alban-Vorstadt. Pass the Kunstmuseum and turn left along Elisabethenstrasse. (Take a look at Theaterplatz, especially its Tinguely Fountain, behind the church on your right.) **Haus Zum Kirschgarten** (Tues, Thur, Fri, Sun 10am–5pm, Wed 10am–8pm, Sat 1–5pm), on the left at Nos 27–29, gives a slice of middle-class Basel life in the 19th century. Built in the late 18th century, it was the home of a wealthy Basel silk ribbon manufacturer, J.R. Burckhardt. Rooms are furnished in the style of the period and there are fine collections of porcelain, Basel silver and scientific instruments.

In the evening, Barfüsserplatz and the streets off the square in the old town, which have lots of interesting bars and restaurants, come alive. For vegetarian fare try Gleich, Steinenvorstadt 23. If you have more time in Basel, a trip to the port from the ferry station on the west bank, between Johanniterbrücke and Dreirosenbrücke, makes for an interesting excursion.

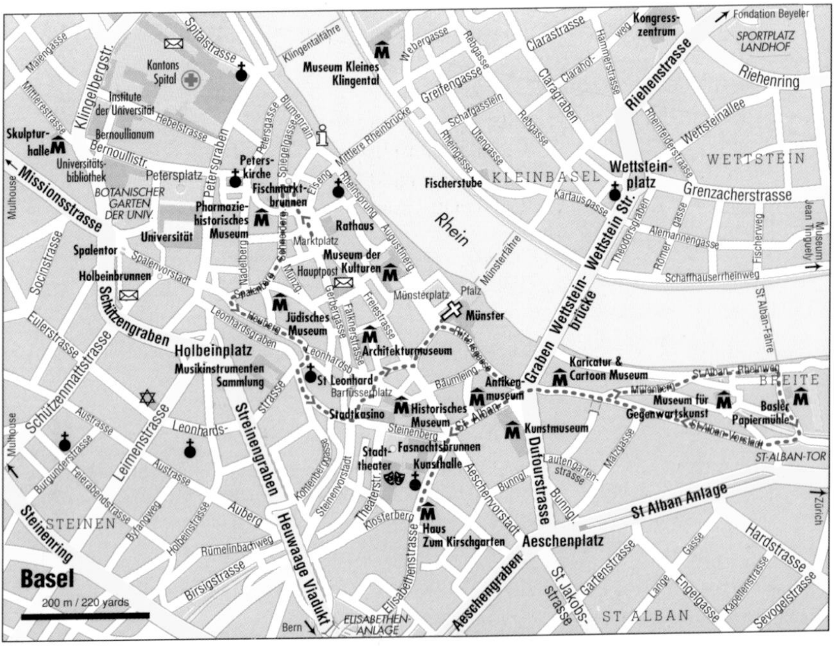

10. Around Lake Lucerne *(see map, p44)*

Lucerne and its surrounding countryside constitute the heartland of Switzerland, both from a geographical and a historical perspective. Lucerne is a small, pretty city and its picturesque setting on Lake Lucerne (Vierwaldstätter See), overlooked by the nearby peaks of Mt Pilatus and Mt Rigi, is one of quintessentially Swiss views. Of the interesting sights in the surrounding region, Schwyz, with its history of mercenaries and the Swiss Charter of 1291 (marking the inception of the country) should not be missed. Two or three days based in Lucerne is ideal.

Lucerne is compact and not as hilly as many of Switzerland's cities. The train network around the region is extensive and there are cogwheel trains and cable cars to the nearby peaks. Paddle steamers operate on Lake Lucerne and it is easy to construct day itineraries combining modes of transport to allow as much, or as little, strenuous walking as you like. You might want to take advantage of a wide choice of ready-made tours that are available from the tourist information office close to the railway station.

If you're staying on the north shore, start the day with a walk along the quays. You will pass a succession of grand hotels and the casino; the views around the lake and to the nearby peaks are magical, with early morning mists sometimes adding to the impression. Behind the lakeside promenade you will see the twin towers of the city's cathedral – the **Collegiate Church of St Leodegar**. This has been a religious site since the 8th century, when a Benedictine monastery was founded here. The church dates from 1645, following a fire that destroyed all but the twin towers of the previous building. It is a fine example of Renaissance style with Italianate cloisters and a grand organ. If you walk up Löwenstrasse and take the lift on the left side of Löwenplatz you will be able to wend your way down into the old town, passing the Musegg Wall. This is part of the old city wall, and features a series of turreted towers dating back to 1386.

The Old Town

Wander through the narrow streets and lanes of the **old town**. Here you will find a range of shops and cafés and impressive squares, such as Weinmarkt and Kornmarkt, with medieval fountains and fine historic frescoes. The **Picasso Museum** (Apr–Oct: 10am–6pm; Nov–Mar: 11am–1pm, 2–4pm) on Furrengasse, next to the Town Hall (Rathaus), features a wonderful collection of works from the last 20 years of Picasso's life, together with a series of revealing photographs, by David Douglas Duncan, of the man considered to be the greatest artist of the 20th century.

Rathaus Quai is the centre of the twice-weekly morning market (Saturday and Tuesday) which is a great place for buying local cheeses and breads.

Above Left: Haus Zum Kirschgarten evokes life in 19th-century Basel
Right: one of Lucerne's many weird and wonderful fountains

Lucerne's most famous landmark, **Kapellbrücke**, stretches across the Reuss River from Rathaus Quai. This covered wooden bridge, built in 1333, with a large water tower in the middle, marks the ancient city boundary. The paintings by Heinrich Wägmann on the roof timbers depict scenes from the region's history. In 1993 a fire devastated a long section of the bridge, but in true Swiss style it has been meticulously restored. Once the moss has grown on the new tiles it will be difficult to spot the join.

There are numerous places for lunch on and around the river banks – try Hotel Restaurant Schiff, Unter der Egg 8, on the north bank, which specialises in fish dishes. If you're on the south bank, Opus, Bahnhofstrasse 16, has a riverside terrace for coffee and snacks. There are lots of shops and eateries on the south bank, and a number of interesting sights, including the baroque Jesuit Church. The **Historisches Museum Luzern** (Tues–Fri 10am–noon, 2–5pm, Sat–Sun 10am–5pm), close to Spreuerbrücke, is a handsome building on the bank of the river. It has some fine military exhibits and reconstructions of rooms furnished in period style as well as a goldsmith's workshop.

Spreuerbrücke is a slightly later construction than Kapellbrücke; it was completed in 1408 and has more interesting features, including Kaspar Meglinger's *Dance of Death* series of paintings dating to 1635. From the bridge you can see a mid-19th-century device known as 'water spikes' for regulating the flow of water for mills. Cross Spreuerbrücke to return to the old town.

Penny Farthings to Airliners

The **Transport Museum** (Apr–Oct: 9am–6pm; Nov–Mar: 10am–5pm) at Lidostrasse 5, a little way out of town along Haldenstrasse (take bus Nos 6 or 8), has lots of exhibits, from penny farthings to airliners. The museum's interactive displays and film shows make it a suitable diversion for children, and for adults seeking a break from the serious contemplation of art and architecture. There is easily enough to see to fill a half-day excursion, and there is a restaurant. When it comes to dinner, Wirtshaus Taube, Burgerstrasse 3, on the south bank serves fine traditional food and is especially cosy in the cold winter months.

There are lots of exciting options for excursions around Lucerne. You can organise trips to last anything from a few hours to a whole day, and it's quite possible to select routes with views of the glorious landscapes which you have probably admired from the city's sundry vantage points.

The **Richard Wagner Museum** (mid-Mar–Nov: Tues–Sun 10am–noon, 2–5pm) is set in a beautiful villa at Tribschen, on the south shore of the lake. It can be reached via bus Nos 6, 7 and 8 and, in summer, by boat. The composer lived here from 1866 to 1872, and it was here that he married Franz Liszt's daughter, Cosima. The museum's exhibits include a collection of 17th-, 18th- and 19th-century musical instruments.

Above: nostalgia at the Transport Museum. **Above Right:** the skier's friend
Right: the covered, wooden Kapellbrücke (bridge) is Lucerne's No 1 landmark

Mt Pilatus and Mt Rigi

You cannot fail to miss the towering peaks of Mt Pilatus and Mt Rigi, which are south and east of the city respectively. Both are less than 10km (6 miles) from the centre of town and their proximity, together with the pretty lakeside setting of Lucerne, make for dramatic views from the shore and a good day's excursion. If you feel like a hike you can opt to walk up or down part of the trails to the summits. Alternatively, various forms of transport will take you from the city to the peak and back. You might want to get a comprehensive package from the tourist information office at Zentralstrasse 5 just behind the station.

Mt Pilatus is 2,120-m (6,950-ft) high and the views it affords of the surrounding region and the Alps to the south are spectacular. The best option in the summer is to take a boat from Lucerne to Alpnachstad, then the cogwheel railway (closed Dec–Apr) to the peak. This is the steepest railway of its kind in the world and in places the gradient is almost 50 percent. There are hotels and restaurants at the top, if you haven't brought a picnic. Cable cars, in three sections, take you down the north slope to Kriens, where you can get a bus (No 1) back to town. The cable cars operate all year round. It is quite feasible to walk all or part of the route down, or up, the northern slope. Likewise the southern route, which you can take from Alpnach or Hergiswil, is accessible on foot. Generally you should allow around five hours for the ascent and three or four hours for the downhill trek.

The sister peak to Mt Pilatus is **Mt Rigi**. At 1,800m (5,900ft) it doesn't quite scale the same heights but it is altogether more alpine in appearance, with more grassy meadows and fewer rocky outcrops. And it still gives great views over a huge expanse of central Switzerland. This was a much-

appreciated spot among the first 19th-century tourists to Switzerland, who initiated the tradition of climbing the peak to see the sunrise. There are various ways of getting up to the peak, apart from walking. One popular long route is to take a boat to Vitznau, then the cogwheel railway to the summit. The railway has been here since 1871, when it became the first mountain route in Europe built to cater to the needs of the growing numbers of visitors. On the way down take the train back as far as Rigi Kaltbad and the cable car down to Weggis, from where you can get a boat or a bus back to Lucerne. As is the case on Mt Pilatus, there is a hotel and restaurant at the top.

Around Lake Lucerne & Lake Zug

A leisurely day's drive around the region is full of small-scale delights. Take the lake route via Meggen and Kussnacht to Cham and on to **Zug**, which is a pretty little town at the northern end of Zuger See. Zug's old town is especially attractive. Of its many fine features, you should see the medieval clock tower (Zytturm), the Fischmarkt and Kolinplatz. Continue down the lakeside to Arth and take the road to Goldau and Schwyz. The road skirts the southern shore of Lauerzer See and is lined with cherry orchards, hence the name Kirschstrasse. At Lauerzer look at the **Z'Graggen Kirsch Distillery** and shop, with its various cherry and other liqueurs.

Schwyz, the next stop, is a delightful town with a couple of important attractions. It is famous for giving Switzerland its name and flag, and was one of the three forest cantons that formed an alliance in the 13th century in a successful attempt to exercise more control over their local government than had been allowed by the Habsburgs. It is believed that the pact was signed in Rütli Meadow, over the water from Brunnen. The Swiss Charter of Confederation of 1291 that commemorates this pact is housed in the **Bundesbriefmuseum** (May–Oct: Tues–Fri 9–11.30am, 1.30–5pm, Sat–Sun 9am–5pm; Nov–Apr: Tues–Sun 1.30–5pm). The subsequent history of the Swiss Confederation is explored here.

Schwyz is also famous for a rather unusual product – soldiers of fortune. The fighting skills of the region's mercenaries were prized by numerous European royal houses from the 16th–18th century. Fighting could be a lucrative profession and many soldiers returned to build fine houses in their home towns. **Ital Reding Hofstatt** (mid-Apr–mid-Nov: Tues–Fri 2–5pm, Sat–Sun 10am–noon, 2–5pm) on Rickenbachstrasse on the edge of town is one such grand mansion, built in baroque style.

The road back to Lucerne clings faithfully to the lake shore and passes through the elegant resort towns of Brunnen, Vitznau and Weggis. You could stop at any one of them and find attractive diversions. From **Brunnen** you can take a short boat ride to Rütli Meadow.

Above: outside Ital Reding Hofstatt

Eastern Switzerland

11. Zürich *(see map, p55)*

Zürich is the economic capital of Switzerland as well as its largest city. Its old town straddles the Limmat River; the picturesque streets and the tree-lined quays are made for strolling, with medieval buildings and a number of museums as a focus. Bahnhofstrasse, Zürich's main commercial thoroughfare, acts as the old town's western boundary and offers the ultimate shopping experience. With more time, a couple of attractions beyond the centre – the Rietberg Museum's Oriental art and the Lindt & Sprüngli Chocolate Museum – are recommended.

The sights of the old town can all be covered in a day, criss-crossing the river via its many bridges. Much of it is pedestrianised. The outlying sights can be reached by a short bus or tram ride from Bahnhofstrasse or Bürkliplatz.

Zürich's origins were as a Roman customs post and hill fort. The settlement on the banks of the Limmat River just to the north of Lake Zürich grew, and by the Middle Ages it was a thriving merchant city. In the 14th century the powerful guilds took over the administration of the city – their power and wealth can be seen in the many ancient guildhalls that dot the old town. In the 16th century Ulrich Zwingli and Jean Calvin led the Reformation, promoting the Protestant work ethic that has contributed to Switzerland's reputation as one of the world's most successful economies.

Innovative Outlook

Zürich's stock exchange was founded in 1877 and today is the fourth largest in the world. The financial expertise concentrated in the city is legendary, and the city's bankers and money managers influence economic activities throughout the world. The intact old town forms the hub for tourists, but the city also has state-of-the-art modern architecture and technological enterprises. With a marked penchant for new and innovative design, the city and its people have a forward-looking ethos that has helped make it the country's largest and best-known metropolis.

The **Schweizerisches Landesmuseum** (Tues–Sun 10am–5pm) is a good place to start a tour of the old town. Housed in a pretty castle-like building sitting on a promontory where the Limmat River is joined by

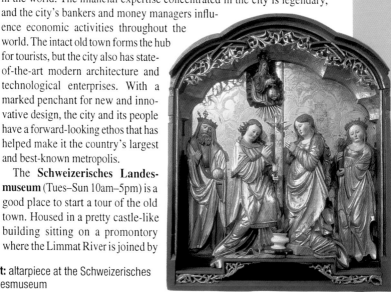

Right: altarpiece at the Schweizerisches Landesmuseum

the Sihl, the exhibitions attempt to explain Switzerland's complex historical and cultural tapestry. Art and artefacts, furniture, costumes and scientific instruments all contribute, through the chronologically arranged galleries, to provide a rich picture of Switzerland through the ages.

Taking Walchebrücke over the river and turning right, follow the river down Limmatquai to the **Rathaus** (Town Hall) built out over the water, and the 13th-century **Zunfthaus Zum Rüden** (Guildhall). The latter has a restaurant with a magnificent vaulted ceiling on the first floor. This is just one of Zürich's many guildhalls that evoke the power of the guilds which governed the city in the 14th and 15th centuries. Today the guilds are not much in evidence, but on the third Monday in April, guild members in traditional costumes parade and burn an effigy of a snowman – symbolising winter's end. The parade ends at Sechseläuten Square; the event is called Sechseläuten.

'Pray and Work'

The austere **Grossmünster** (mid-Mar–Oct: daily 9am–6pm; Nov–mid-Mar: 10am–4pm) cathedral was completed in the 13th century and is the place where Ulrich Zwingli began the Reformation in the early 16th century. His preachings included the instruction to 'pray and work' – a motto which set the tone for Zürich life long after his death. The gorgeously colourful stained-glass windows in the choir were created by Augusto Giacometti in 1932. The interior of the minster is remarkably plain, though there is some nice detailing in the Romanesque sculpture on the capitals.

Follow Münstergasse, turn right into Rindermarkt and right again up the

small Reh-Gässchen alley at the start of Neumarkt. Follow this round to the right and turn left up Untere Zäune towards Heimplatz. Before visiting Zürich's Fine Arts Museum, the Kunsthaus, it might be time for lunch. The fine Florhof restaurant, at the nearby Florhofgasse 4, has a lovely garden terrace in summer – go left at the top of Untere Zäune, cross over the main road, and Florhofgasse is directly ahead.

The **Kunsthaus** (Tues–Thur 10am–9pm, Fri–Sun 10am–5pm) is back on Heimplatz. Modern art is well represented here by Monet, Picasso, Bacon and Hockney among others, and there are collections of works by Giacometti and Chagall. There is also fine religious art from earlier centuries.

Now wind your way back down towards the river via Winkelwiese, Trittligasse, Frankengasse, Neustadtgasse, left down Kirchgasse and back along Limmatquai, turning left over Münsterbrücke. From this point you can see the towers of St Peter's Church (notice the clock face, which is the largest in Europe) and also the Fraumünster. The **Fraumünster** (May–Sep: Mon–Sat 9am–6pm; Oct and Mar–Apr: Mon–Sat 10am–5pm; Nov–Feb: 10am–4pm, Sun 2–6pm) dates from the 12th century and has lovely Romanesque cloisters. The Russian-French artist Marc Chagall created the stained-glass windows in the choir and south transept in 1970.

A Famous Shopping Street

Take Storchengasse and go left up Strehlgasse and Pfalzgasse which brings you up to **Lindenhof**. This small wooded hill marks the spot where a Roman customs post was built, thus founding the city of Turicum, today Zürich. Great views of the city can be had from this small park. Continue through the park and take Fortunagasse down to the left into the newer part of town. Turn left up Rennweg, and right down Widdergasse and right again down Augustinergasse, which has some very attractive old shop fronts. This brings you down into **Bahnhofstrasse** – one of the most famous shopping streets in the world.

Examples of cutting-edge modern architecture sit side by side with elegant Art Nouveau facades dotted with rows of lime trees. Here you will find an impressive array of designer labels and expensive art and antiques. There are some affordable stores, particularly at the northern end (close to the train station) and in neighbouring streets such as Schweizergasse, Löwenplatz, Seidengasse and also Rennweg, including department stores such as Jelmoli.

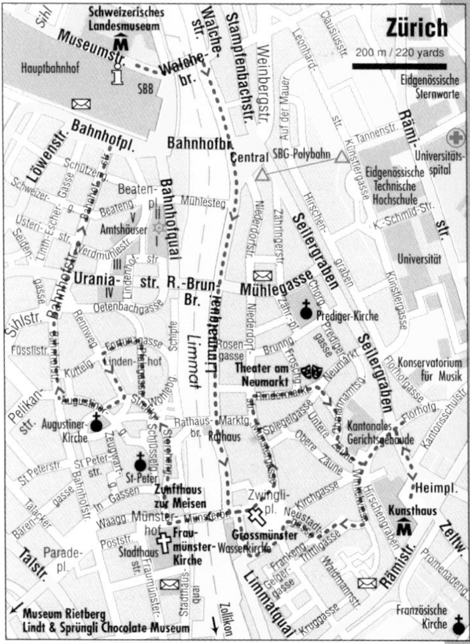

Top Left: Giacometti stained glass
Left: Bahnhofstrasse mannequins

Many Swiss banks also have establishments off Bahnhofstrasse, and it is in their vaults, not open to the public, that vast wealth is reputed to lie.

If you have more time in Zürich there are a couple of museums that lie beyond the old town which are well worth a visit. Both the Rietberg Museum and the Lindt & Sprüngli Chocolate Museum are only a short tram ride southwest of the old town, off Seestrasse. Trams 161 and 165 from Bürkliplatz and 7 from Paradeplatz along Bahnhofstrasse will drop you close to both. The **Rietberg Museum** (Tues–Sun 10am–5pm) is housed in a beautiful old villa set in parkland just south of Lake Zürich. The collections, which focus on Asian-Pacific art, have wonderful Indian, Javanese, Khmer and Chinese statues, and also Japanese prints.

It was once possible to tour the Lindt & Sprüngli factory to see how the chocolate was made. Unfortunately, due to hygiene regulations, these tours have now ceased but next to the factory, the small **Lindt & Sprüngli Chocolate Museum** (Wed–Fri 10am–noon, 1–4pm) at Seestrasse 204 offers the next best thing – exhibits about chocolate and its manufacture, and a free box of chocolates.

There are any number of bars and restaurants throughout the old town and on the quays. The roads between Limmatquai and Niederdorf in particular have a good choice, and there's a very lively atmosphere in the evenings in this part of town. Adler's Swiss Chuchi at Rosengasse 10 serves lots of traditional Swiss fare.

12. Along the Rhine *(see map, p58)*

The stretch of the Rhine flowing west from Lake Constance in the country's northern tip is the most beautiful, with lovely falls and historic towns and villages such as Stein am Rhein and Schaffhausen.

Schaffhausen and Stein am Rhein, 20km (12 miles) apart, are both easily reached by car or train from Zürich, and in summer you can sail along the Rhine between Stein am Rhein and Schaffhausen – this is a wonderful hour and a half journey and much the most scenic part of the Rhine. If you make an early start and take a boat from Stein am Rhein mid-morning you can do the whole itinerary in a day. There's an hourly train between Schaffhausen and Stein am Rhein if you've left a car at either town.

Stein am Rhein

The small town of Stein am Rhein, situated at the point where the Rhine leaves Lake Constance, is an absolute jewel, but get there early because it is not very big and it's a much-visited spot that features on the itinerary of many coach tours. **Rathausplatz** is outstanding; it has many beautifully painted 16th-century houses studded with fine oriel windows, and it makes a good focal point. Each house has a name, for example Pelican House and the Sun Inn, and their frescoes artfully illustrate the individual themes. **Understadt** is also

Above: the Rietberg Museum, Zürich. **Above right:** an oriel window in Stein am Rhein
Right: Rathausplatz's 16th-century houses

overflowing with fine buildings and pretty fountains. The **Museum Lindwurm** (Mar–Oct: Wed–Mon 10am–5pm) at Understadt 18 recreates the elegant interiors of a substantial 19th-century townhouse and also presents the range of activities that would have been undertaken by both the owners and servants of such a house.

Medieval Schaffhausen

Schaffhausen is one of the loveliest old towns in the country, and although the old fortifications are largely gone, with the exception of one or two towers on the western side, the impressive guildhalls, winding narrow lanes and splendid patrician dwellings with their oriel windows give a strong impression of a medieval town. There are plenty of artfully facaded houses to admire as you wander the ancient streets, but a couple to look out for are **Haus Zum Ritter** (House of the Knight) on Vordergasse, with its colourful frescoes illustrating knightly exploits, and **Haus Zum Steinbock** on Oberstadt, decorated with rich stucco work. Vordergasse is the heart of town with a market on Tuesdays and Saturdays and many interesting shops.

Schaffhausen has long been an important trading and transport centre because of the Rhine Falls 3km (2 miles) downstream, which even today are too great an obstacle for shipping. Boats sailing between Lake Constance and Basel, further down the Rhine, have to unload their cargoes and load up again beyond the falls. The town became a religious centre in the 11th century when Count Eberhard von Nellenburg founded a Benedictine monastery – **All Saints** (Tues–Sun 10am–noon, 2–5pm).

Wander round this peaceful complex with its Romanesque cathedral, pretty cloisters, medieval herb garden and **Museum zu Allerheiligen** (Tues–Sat

noon–5pm, Thur till 8pm, Sun 11am–5pm). This museum has a wide variety of exhibits including some splendid religious art. **Munot Fort** (May–Sep: daily 8am–8pm, Oct–Apr: daily 9am–5pm), towering over the old town at the eastern end, is a rare example of a circular keep. Today the 9pm watch is still rung – a reminder of the days when the town's gates were closed at night.

Europe's Largest Falls

A very popular trip from Schaffhausen is to see the nearby **Rhine Falls** – Europe's largest. Stretching across 150m (492ft) and dropping 23m (75ft) the falls are truly spectacular. It takes less than an hour to walk along the riverside from the town to reach them, or there is an hourly train to Schloss Laufen south of the falls. If you feel like experiencing the power of the water at close quarters, take one of the many boat trips that operate in summer from the jetties in the town.

If you have time, the best way to see the region around Schaffhausen is to take a boat trip from Stein am Rhein down the Rhine to Schaffhausen. You can choose from large modern boats or traditional *weidlingen*, and there are a number of scheduled and excursion services. En route downstream look out for some pretty settlements, such as Diessenhofen and Bibermühle.

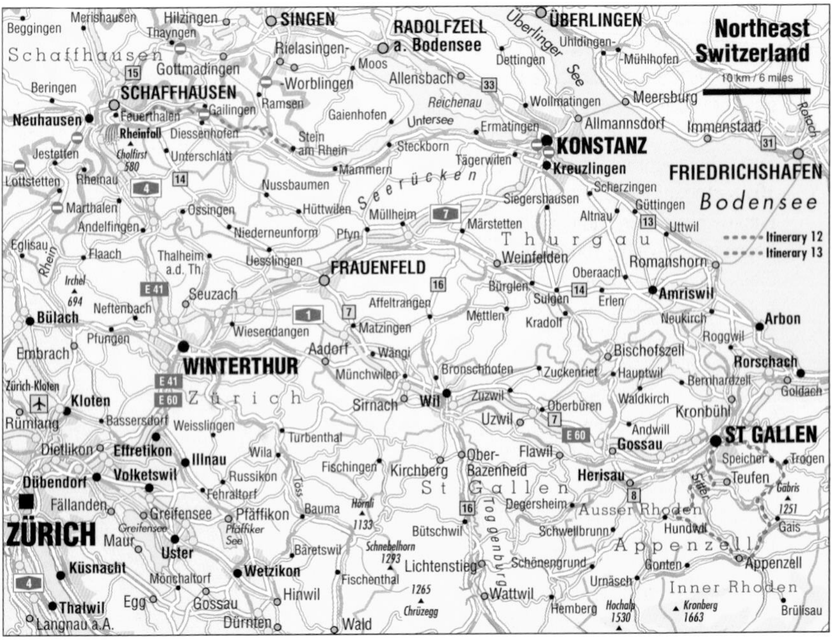

13. St Gallen and Appenzellerland *(see map, p58)*

The combination of St Gallen's handsome city architecture and ancient religious sights, and the rolling hillsides, strong pastoral tradition and quaint country towns and villages of Appenzellerland makes for an interesting and varied two-day itinerary.

St Gallen is a major city close to the German and Austrian border that is easily accessible by train. All the sights within the city are within walking distance of each other, and a day will allow you to visit most of the major ones. From here it is possible to visit the town of Appenzell by train and Stein and Trogen by bus, but it is much easier to explore the countryside by car.

St Gallen is the country's seventh-largest city and a major food-processing and textile centre. In the 7th century, an Irish monk named Gallus stumbled and fell in the forest. Interpreting this as a sign from God to stay put he built a hermit's cell. In the next century a Benedictine monastery was built and the development of the city began. St Gallen was a vital focal point of religious education in the Middle Ages and after the Reformation became an industrial centre concentrating on textiles and agriculture. As the town grew it colonised the nearby hills – most of the major sights are at the foot of these low hills in the heart of the city – the old town. Due to its peripheral location and its lack of traditional Swiss staples – mountains and lakes (though Lake Constance is just to the north) – it is often overlooked as a tourist destination. In some ways this makes it even more appealing – the city's architecture and gently rolling agricultural lands to the south are delightful.

A Religious Centre

The unmissable sights of the old town are in the Cathedral and Abbey Library complex which lies on the southern side, on the site of the original monastery. The vast **Cathedral** (Mon–Sat 9am–6pm, Sun noon–5.30pm) dates from 1768 and is pure baroque. The lavish interior decoration includes paintings on the central dome ceiling by Joseph Wannenmacher. The stalls and confessionals are also particularly fine. The interior of the cathedral contrasts strikingly with the exterior which is plain and austere.

The main hall of the **Abbey Library** (Apr–Oct: Mon–Sat 10am–5pm, Sun 10am–4pm; Dec–Mar: Mon–Sat 10am–noon, 1.30–5pm; closed Nov) is a fantastic rococo creation, built in 1767 and housing some of the 100,000 rare and precious religious manuscripts and early books in its collection. Some date to the 8th century. The marble and wood shelves, rich, delicate plaster, painted ceiling, and grand parquet floor are so overwhelmingly ornate that even serious readers would be hard-pressed not to be distracted.

The streets of the old town, a few steps away from the cathedral, feature attractive buildings with oriel windows and

Above Left: the Rhine Falls
Right: a carved door in the Abbey Library

elaborately carved door frames. At Gallusstrasse 22 the **Zum Greif** house has a fine baroque oriel window and murals. **Haus Zum Pelikan**, Schmiedgasse 15, has carvings representing the continents; Spisergasse and Marktgasse have similar treasures. The old town is especially lively on Wednesday, Friday and Saturday mornings when produce markets are held on Marktgasse. Shopping is good in the old town – linen and embroidered items are attractive buys.

Haus Zum Pelikan serves a good selection of inexpensive meals. Try the local beer for which St Gallen is famous. After lunch take Multergasse and cross over Oberer Graben to Vadianstrasse to the **Textilmuseum** (Mon–Sat 10am–noon, 2–5pm, Sun 10am–5pm). This museum concentrates on St Gallen's tradition of producing textiles and embroidery, from the early manufacture and trade of linen in the 15th century to the more recent trade in lace and cotton goods.

Appenzellerland

The area between St Gallen and Mt Säntis, 20km (12 miles) to the south, and east as far as the Rhine (the border with Austria) is known as Appenzellerland. It is a region of rolling green hills and rich pastures, and it has remained a quiet, independent community of small rural villages with old traditions and a strong sense of identity.

In the villages *Landsgemeinden* still prevails – issues affecting individual towns are decided on a show of hands in the main square. This happens once a year, or every two years in Appenzell and Trogen.

Above: Abbey Library interior
Left: house facade in Appenzellerland

Dairy farming is vital – the region is famed for its strong, rich Appenzell cheese. This part of Switzerland is also rich in local crafts, particularly painting, weaving and embroidery. Painting the all-important herds of cows *(senntumsmalerei),* usually being led to or from mountain pastures, is a tradition that goes back three centuries; you will see old and modern examples of this delightful art form displayed in the museums, restaurants and shops of the region.

Folk Museums

Heading south out of St Gallen, take the road towards Teufen. Just before you reach Teufen there's a right turn to **Stein**. This little village, situated on a rise above the surrounding countryside, features the small **Appenzeller Volkskunde Museum** (Folk Museum; Mon 1.30–5pm, Tues–Sat 10am–noon, 1.30–5pm, Sun 10am–5pm). Here, traditional artefacts of everyday use are displayed along with some of the arts and crafts of the region, including painted wooden panels, weaving and ornamental beltmaking and carpentry. There is a local cheese-making dairy, the **Appenzell Schaukäserie** (May–Oct: 9am–7pm; Nov–Apr: 9am–6pm), next door with demonstrations between 9 and 11am.

Continue on and turn left at the main road to **Appenzell**, the main town of the region. It's extremely attractive and can, in summer, be overrun with busloads of tourists. The pretty centre is filled with traditional wooden painted houses – the front facades a mass of small windows all with the same curtains. The streets invite you to wander around and there are plenty of gift shops, some selling local products such as embroidery and cheese. The **Appenzell Museum** (Apr–Oct: daily 10am–noon, 2–5pm; Nov–Mar: Tues–Sun 2–4pm), situated next to the town hall, is a folk museum containing lovely local art, both painting and lace work. Appenzell has lots of lunch options.

From Appenzell, take the road to Gais, then back towards Teufen. If you turn off to the right after 2km (1¼ miles) along a minor road you will reach **Trogen**, another typical Appenzellerland settlement. It is known for the *Landsgemeinden* that takes place in even years, usually during April, in the central square (Landsgemeindeplatz). The square is surrounded by handsome mansions built in the 17th and 18th centuries by merchants and farmers.

Appenzellerland is a good venue for hiking and skiing away from the big resorts of the Valais. The Alpstein range, south of Appenzell, with Säntis its highest peak (2,500m/8,200ft), offers good hiking routes. Mt Säntis itself is a challenging walk, but there is a cable car, from which the view encompasses Lake Constance to the north and the Bernese Alps to the south. The slopes of the nearby Mt Kronberg (1,660m/5,445ft) offer good, quiet ski slopes in winter, and the welcoming small towns and villages of Appenzellerland provide ideal retreats for recuperating after a day's exercise.

Above: painting at the Appenzell Museum

14. Graubünden *(see map, p65)*

The canton of Graubünden in eastern Switzerland is the country's largest. With the exception of its famous winter resorts, which include Davos, Klosters and St Moritz, it remains relatively off the beaten track. The upper reaches of the Rhine, via one or two spectacular gorges, flow through Graubünden, and the Engadine Valley in the east is one of the most delightful alpine areas in the whole country. Chur, the canton's capital and where this tour begins, is an ancient settlement with an attractive old town.

Chur and the Engadine Valley are easily accessible by train. However, given that so much of the canton's appeal lies in its natural beauty, it's far easier and more rewarding to explore the region in a car. This is an expansive area that has little in the way of motorways, so if you are planning to see the Engadine and the Swiss National Park, and take in a few hours in Chur, you should consider a two- or three-day stay as the minimum.

The city of **Chur** claims to be the oldest settlement in Switzerland, with a history going back 2,000 years, and there is evidence of human habitation in the area as far back as 3000BC. It has long been significant as a consequence of its important strategic location in the Rhine Valley – a vital trade and military route – linking the German powers in northern Europe with those of Italy, and also as a religious centre. The small old town has winding streets and small squares flanked by imposing town houses.

The Romanesque and Gothic **Cathedral** (daily 8am–7pm), dating back to the 12th century, is quietly impressive. Its most splendid treasure is the carved and gilded wooden Gothic triptych (the largest in the country) by Jakob Russ. Next to the cathedral you will find the **Bishop's Palace** which unfortunately is not open to the public. The palace was built in 1732 and still

Above: Gothic altar in Chur Cathedral

functions as the seat of the Bishop of Chur. Just below, the **Rätisches Museum** (Tues–Sun 10am–noon, 2–5pm), situated in a fine 17th-century town house, constitutes the local history museum. Located in the very heart of the old town, nestling in the shadow of the Cathedral and the Bishop's Palace, Reichsgasse is one of the most attractive streets and opens out onto a fine square, Arcas, which is full of cafés.

Walk just a few hundred metres up Poststrasse and you will come to the **Bünder Kunstmuseum** (Tues–Sun 10am–noon, 2–5pm, Thur till 8pm), on Postplatz. The fine arts on display here focus on the works of 18th-, 19th- and 20th-century artists associated with the region, most notably the Giacometti family – Giovanni, Augusto and Alberto. For lunch, try Hofkellerie, Hof 1 (closed Mon), just down from the cathedral. It serves a number of regional specialities such as *bündnerfleisch* (paper-thin air-dried beef) and *bündner gerstensuppe* (beef and vegetable soup).

Rhine Gorge

Between Reichenau and Flims, **Rheinschlucht**, 15km (10 miles) to the west of Chur, is an impressive sight, where the powerful upper waters of the Rhine have channelled a deep gorge. The 12-km (8-mile) walk from Reichenau to the gorge and back makes for a good afternoon (or whole day) ramble. If you're into more exhilarating sports, river rafting at Reichenau is available to those willing to pit their wits against the speeding waters of the Rhine.

St Moritz

St Moritz is one of the best-known ski resorts in the world, and today it is famous for being famous. Indeed St Moritz is synonymous with the lifestyle glamorous international celebrities, royalty and the merely wealthy. As far back as Roman times it was well known for the curative powers of its spring waters, and later as a summer recreation area, but it wasn't until the mid-1860s, when a group of English visitors came to enjoy the winter sun and started skiing and tobogganing, that the winter resort par excellence took off.

Today St Moritz is an extremely cosmopolitan resort with high-rise hotels and lots of designer shops to complement the natural attractions. The town comprises St Moritz Dorf, to the north of the lake, which is the centre of the ski resort, and St Moritz Bad – the health spa side of town. In terms of winter sports St Moritz offers all the facilities you can imagine.

The town is home to the world's first ski school, which was established in 1927, and the world-famous Cresta Run. In winter the lake, as well as the slopes, are a focus of activity, with golf, curling

Right: exclusive St Moritz

and sledge-racing all taking place on the frozen water. In summer St Moritz's nearby peak, Piz Nair (3,057m/10,027ft), and the surrounding slopes of the Upper Engadine Valley, offer great views and hiking. With the network of trails, cable cars and lots of local hamlets you can take walks ranging from the gentle to the strenuous. In the town, the **Engadine Museum** (Mon–Fri 10am–noon, 2–5pm, Sun 10am–noon) is worth visiting for its splendid displays on local history, culture and architecture.

Lower Engadine Valley

The Lower Engadine Valley has a far lower profile than its glitzy neighbour, St Moritz, to the west. The valley of the Inn (or En) River contains a number of natural and cultural jewels. The wooded lower slopes, exposed screes and limestone peaks, and tranquil, traditional villages of the valley are less dramatic than much of the Swiss Alps but no less appealing, and for nature lovers and hikers they offer a wealth of wildlife. The valley is one of the few remaining regions where the Romansch language is still spoken – though German and English are widely understood.

Zernez is a small town at the start of the Lower Engadine Valley. One of the town's functions is as an entry point to the **Swiss National Park** (Jun–Oct: 8.30am–6pm, Tues 8.30am–10pm). You can obtain information about the park, including local accommodation and recommended walks, from the National Park house in Zernez. Established in 1914, this is the only national park in the country. All human interference is forbidden; drivers are obliged to keep to the one main route (the Ofenpass road) through the park, and hikers to the 80km (50 miles) of trails. As a result of this policy of 'neglect', fauna and flora are abundant, with marmots and chamois easily spotted, and the landscape is wild, and at times bleak. The official guided walks, conducted on Tuesdays and Thursdays, are worth taking.

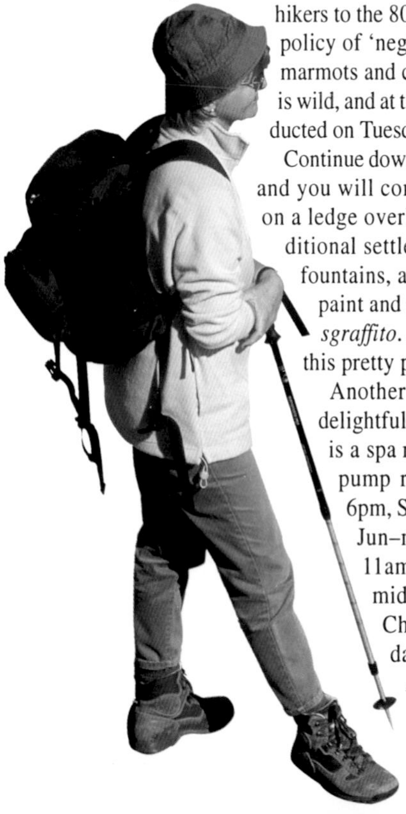

Continue down the Engadine Valley for 15km (10 miles) and you will come to the lovely little town of **Guarda**, on a ledge overlooking the valley. This is a typical traditional settlement, with narrow cobbled streets and fountains, and stone-built houses gaily decorated in paint and plaster in a technique which is known as *sgraffito*. Allow about an hour for an amble round this pretty place.

Another 15 km (10 miles) on is **Tarasp**. This delightful village with an imposing castle *(schloss)* is a spa resort and you can take the waters at the pump room (May–Oct: Mon–Fri 7–10am, 4–6pm, Sat 7–10am). **Schloss Tarasp** (tours only; Jun–mid-Jul: 2.30pm; mid-Jul–mid-Aug: 11am, 2.30pm, 3.30pm and 4.30pm; mid-Aug–mid-Oct: 2.30pm and 3.30pm; Christmas–Easter Tues and Thur 4.30pm) dates from 1040 and for centuries was an Austrian stronghold. At the start of the

Left: be sure to have the right hiking gear
Above right: Schloss Tarasp

19th century the estate was integrated into Graubünden; today the castle is a private residence. It was restored at the beginning of the 20th century and in addition to its fine architecture and location it has a great collection of antique furniture.

Spa Facilities

A few kilometres on from Tarasp is **Scuol**, the largest of the Lower Engadine Valley towns. Like Tarasp it is an attractive spa town, and it too features the traditional *sgraffito*-decorated houses. Scuol's range of accommodation options makes it an excellent base from which to explore the region. The **Bogn Engiadina Scuol** spa complex (daily 8am–10pm) has a Roman-Irish spa section. There are various treatments and facilities – book in for a two-hour, or longer, session.

As a summer hiking base Scuol is ideal, with the beauty of the natural landscape dotted by the delightful villages of the Engadine. For a pleasant half-day walk you could try the Ftan-Ardez-Guarda-Lavin hike along the ridge, and then take the bus back to Scuol. In winter Scuol's ski slopes are quieter than those of St Moritz, and there are some 60km (37 miles) of cross-country tracks as well as downhill runs.

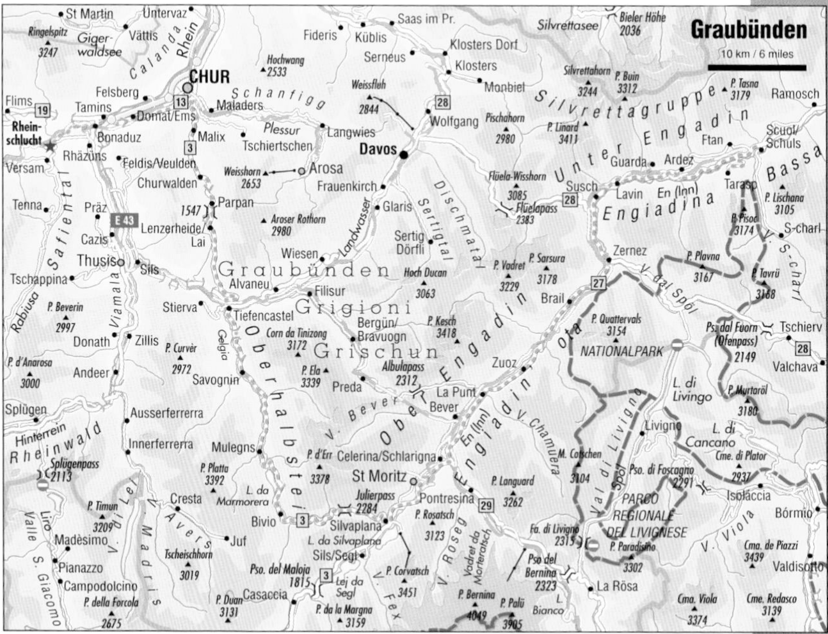

15. The Ticino *(see map, p67)*

The Ticino, in the far south of the country – south of the Alps to the Italian lakes, some of whose northern shores lie within Switzerland – is a very attractive region of Italianate lakeside resorts, majestic mountains and remote pine- and chestnut-clad valleys. The region's language, food, wine, customs and climate are all more redolent of Italy than Switzerland.

You need time – a minimum of three days – and a car to begin to explore the Ticino. There is a motorway, via the Gotthard Pass (and Tunnel) and a railway down to the main cities of Bellinzona, Lugano and Locarno, any one of which will serve as a great base for a stay in the region. To visit the small villages and valleys of the rural area north of the lake shores you will need to take a car or the local buses.

Ticino's origins and development are Italian. The region forged strong links with Lombardy, and this relationship can be seen in some of the architecture and culture. The castles around Bellinzona are testament to its important strategic position on the route to the passes of the Alps. It wasn't until the 16th century that Swiss control began to be exercised, and the canton finally joined the confederation in 1803.

Bellinzona

Bellinzona is the capital of the canton of Ticino and is worth exploring, even if your focus is the lakeside region. The motorway route south goes through Bellinzona so there's no need for a detour. It's a city of castles – three in fact. Of these, **Castelgrande** (Mon–Sun 10am–6pm) with its robust battlements is the oldest and most impressive. It stands on a rock above the

town over which it casts a protective presence. One of the walls stretches right down into the town. The castle was built in the 13th century (though some fortifications date back to the 4th century), and has been added to and restored over the years, most recently in the late 1980s when the entrance and courtyard were renovated and a lift to the town below installed. It was built by the Visconti family, the ruling power during the medieval period, but recent archaeological finds have confirmed that the site was inhabited as far back as 5000BC and again during Roman times.

Lively Piazzas

Piazza Nosetto and **Piazza Collegiata** form the heart of Bellinzona and lie at the foot of the castle. They buzz with life, especially on Saturday morning when the weekly market is in full swing. As well as produce from the region there are usually craft stalls, and the squares are lined with tempting cafés in which you can enjoy a coffee or cappuccino. Via Teatro, leading off the Piazza Nosetto, takes you up to the recently restored neoclassical **Teatro Sociale** – to arrange a visit call the Fondazione, tel: 091-825 4818. It is a beautiful example of a mid-19th-century theatre and today stages concerts and plays. Up Via Nosetto is **Collegiata dei Santi Pietro e Stefano**, a Renaissance church with an imposing pale stone facade, built by Tomaso Rodari, who also designed Como cathedral. It has a fine rose window and some good 18th-century frescoes.

Café Commercianti at Via Teatro 5 is a good central place for lunch and serves particularly delicious ice creams. Bellinzona's other great church lies 1km (½ mile) to the south down Via Lugano. **Santa Maria delle Grazie** (currently closed for restoration) dates from the 15th century and was part of a Franciscan monastery. The church's most outstanding feature is a lavishly painted rood screen depicting the Crucifixion and scenes from the Life of Christ. The frescoes are thought to date from 1505.

Bellinzona's two other castles are also worth exploring, especially if you feel like a short hike. **Castello di Montebello** (Mar–Nov daily 10am–6pm), which stands above Castelgrande, once formed part of the town's defensive walls and is thought to have been built in the 13th or 14th century by the Rusconi family, who came from Como. It was later taken by the Visconti and then, in the centuries of Swiss rule over the region (16th and 17th centuries), it was renamed Castello di Svitto. It has a truly impressive drawbridge and wonderful views.

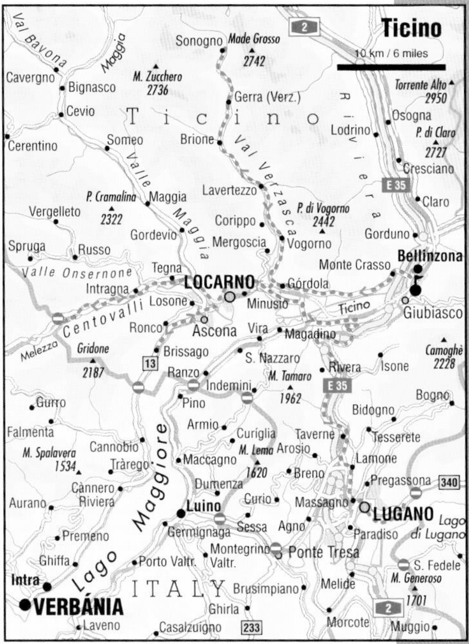

Above Left: Castello di Montebello, with Castello di Sasso Corbaro behind
Left: Castelgrande

Castello di Sasso Corbaro (Mar–Nov: Tues–Sun 10am–6pm) is further east of the town and stands much higher, overlooking the valley. This castle was built in 1479 by the Sforza family, rulers of Milan – after Milanese troops were defeated at the Battle of Giornico – to defend the Ticino Valley. It has had a somewhat chequered history and a number of name changes. After the building fell into a state of disrepair at the end of the 18th century it was taken on by three local families who turned it into a summer residence. It is now owned by the state.

Mediterranean Feel

The lakeside town of **Locarno** at the northern end of Lake Maggiore is quintessentially Mediterranean in atmosphere and appearance, with hot, sunny summers, warm, wet winters and a preponderance of palm trees. The climate is decidedly mild – spring and autumn days are frequently fine and sunny, and the town's parks and gardens make the most of this – Locarno hosts a camellia festival in April.

Piazza Grande is enormous and the heart of town, and bustles with life. The old paved square is a good place to start the day, with breakfast or a coffee at one of the many delightful bars and cafés. For two weeks in early August it is the centre of Locarno's International Film Festival – when the square is transformed into a huge open-air cinema in the evening. The quaint, arcaded old-town streets radiate off the *piazza* to the north and west and these are well worth exploring. Taking Via F Rusca off the western side of the square will bring you to one of Locarno's most famous landmarks, the **Castello Visconteo** (Apr–Oct: Tues–Sun 10am–5pm). The 14th-century building was heavily fortified by Milan's ruling Visconti family. Today you only see a small part of the fortress that stood here before being burnt down in the 16th century. Inside the building is the **Museo Archeologico** which has a good collection of Bronze Age and Roman artefacts, glassware in particular.

Above the old town you will find the sanctuary of **Madonna del Sasso** (Mon–Sat 8am–5pm), a popular destination with sightseeing tourists and devoted pilgrims alike. It can be reached on foot, by car, or by funicular railway from Via della Stazione. Contemplate going either up or down by foot as this is the traditional pilgrim route and you will pass the Stations of the Cross. In 1480 a local monk had a vision of the Virgin Mary on this spot; the first chapel was erected, and subsequently the sanctuary was rebuilt and extended. The striking baroque Church of the Annunciation has some wonderful frescoes and paintings.

Above: Madonna del Sasso sanctuary. **Right:** a Locarno carving. **Far Right**: the sanctuary setting

Cimetta, the 1,670-m (5,478-ft) peak that rises high above Locarno, can be reached quickly and conveniently by cable car and chair lift from Madonna del Sasso, and the views over the lake and valleys to the north are quite fabulous. From here you can ski in the winter or hike down into the Val Verzasca in the summer. When you make your way back to the old town you might like to try Vecchia Locarno, Via della Motta 10, for lunch.

There are plenty of short trips out of town for an afternoon – either by car, bus or boat (the port is close to Piazza Grande). Ronco and Brissago are both ideal destinations or, if you would rather stay in the immediate vicinity, Ascona is only a short bus journey away. **Ronco** is a small, exceedingly pretty, one-time fishing village, with great views out over the lake, and the short drive down the lake shore (8km/5 miles) to reach it is lovely.

Brissago and the Isles of Brissago are a little further away and virtually as far as you can go on the lake while staying within Switzerland's borders. You can take a boat from Locarno or Ascona to get to Brissago which, like Ronco, clings picturesquely to the steep lakeside. San Pancrazio, the larger of the lake's two islands, is now the **Parco Botanico** (Apr–Oct: daily 9am–6pm), Ticino's beautiful botanic gardens. The gardens were developed by a couple of wealthy owners of the islands over the first half of the 20th century and have been open to the public since 1950. Flowers and plants flourish in the mild climate, and the gardens contain a diverse range of subtropical species from all around the world. On the opposite bank of the Maggia River from Locarno is the town of **Ascona**. Once a fishing village, Ascona is today a hive of bars and restaurants, and arts and crafts galleries. The bars and restaurants that you will find lining the old town's narrow lanes and the lakeshore offer plenty of choice and a lively atmosphere for dining in the evenings.

Valleys of the Ticino

The valleys north of Lake Maggiore offer a contrasting view and experience of the canton from the lively cosmopolitan resorts on the lakes. Here you will find beautiful scenery, small rural villages and a much slower pace of life. There is a network of hiking trails throughout the region and, as the main towns of Bellinzona, Locarno and Lugano are all only a short car or bus

trip away, it is quite feasible to undertake a full day's hiking, during which you can explore a very different side of the Ticino.

Centovalli, to the west of Locarno, is the only valley containing a railway line – the connection between Bellinzona and the Italian town of Domodóssola. Hourly trains from Locarno stop at the small villages along Centovalli, 'Valley of a Hundred Valleys', and the ride itself is an extremely scenic one. The railway and the network of trails make it easy to put together a hiking route. There are numerous attractive stone-built villages through which to pass, including Intragna, with a small regional rural life museum, the **Museo Regionale delle Centovalli e del Pedemonte** (Apr–Oct: Tues–Sun 2–6pm); Verdasio with its narrow winding lanes; and Rasa above the valley, which is accessible by cable car from Verdasio. For those in search of local thrills the Centovalli bridge at Intragna is a well-known bungee-jumping spot.

Val Verzasca, to the north of Locarno, is wilder, though very easy to get to by car or bus. The valley is a dead end, and the further up you go the more off the beaten track you get. It is possible to start a walk from Cimetta or from a number of the villages further up the valley. **Corippo**, at the northern end of the Vogorno lake, is a pretty hamlet – a cluster of traditional houses, complete with a slender stone belltower rising over the village – that clings to the slopes of the valley. Just 3km (2 miles) up the valley, Lavertezzo has a charming humped stone bridge, which spans the river and is a renowned local beauty spot. Brione further up the valley and Sonogno at the top end are both attractive villages with beautiful little churches. Both are good starting points for walks.

To Lugano

Lugano, on the shores of the lake of the same name, is the largest of Ticino's towns. The **historic core** of Lugano is a maze of attractive *piazzas* and winding arcaded streets, made for wandering. **Piazza della Riforma**, the main square, is lined with cafés facing the lake and is the site of the local tourist office. In the northwest corner of the old town, the **Cathedral of San Lorenzo** has an imposing white Renaissance facade and interior frescoes. The steep climb up Via Cattedrale or the short funicular ride from Piazza Cioccaro up to the station brings you to the cathedral. The **Museo Cantonale d'Arte** (Wed–Sun 10am–5pm, Tues 2–5pm) on the eastern side of the old town has a good collection of works by Swiss artists, housed in a sumptuous villa. The old town is overflowing with watering holes. Try one of the eateries in or around the Piazza della Riforma for lunch.

Just 2km (1¼ miles) to the east of the old town, along the lake shore, you will find two notable museums, both easily reached either by boat or by bus No 1 from Piazza Manzoni (next to Piazza della Riforma). You arrive at the **Villa Favorita** museum first. In a striking 17th-century villa, complete with beautiful lakeside gardens, the **Foundation Thyssen-Bornemisza**

Above: off the beaten track in the Val Verzasca

(closed until further notice) has a wonderful exhibition of 18th-, 19th- and 20th-century art taken from the Thyssen-Bornemisza family's extensive art collection, amassed over the best part of the 20th century. The **Museo delle Culture Extraeuropee** (Wed–Sun 10am–5pm) housed in the **Villa Heleneum**, a little further along Via Cortiva, contains an interesting collection of artefacts and art from non-European cultures, particularly Southeast Asia and Oceania.

The Rio of the Old Continent

There is no shortage of nearby attractions for half-day excursions. **Monte Brè** and **Monte San Salvatore** lie respectively just to the east and south of town and the latter's distinctive resemblance to Sugarloaf Mountain gives rise to Lugano's nickname – 'the Rio de Janeiro of the Old Continent'. Both towns are accessible by funicular and provide wonderful views and picnic spots.

Gandria is a small town, further east along the lake, close to the Italian border. Visitors usually take a boat to Gandria which, with its colourful houses tumbling down to the water's edge and pretty jetties and lakeside restaurants, is best appreciated from the lake. The town is a maze of narrow lanes and arcaded houses. Apart from soaking up the atmosphere you can take a boat trip to the opposite side of the lake where, housed in a former Swiss customs post, you will find the **Museo Doganale Svizzero** (Apr–Oct: 1.30–5.30pm). This is a fascinating little museum, especially as it posts details of the role these towns and their officers played in World War II.

Above: Piazza della Riforma, Lugano's main square
Right: the grounds of the Villa Favorita

FLOWERS TRADE
MARCEL FISCHER AG

Leisure Activities

SHOPPING

While there is the usual range of international chains and brands in the shopping streets of Switzerland's main towns and cities, there are also plenty of individual family-run establishments offering good quality and excellent service. Most of the country's towns and cities still have unspoilt old towns and it is here that you should find a concentration of interesting boutiques and galleries. When it comes to food and wine, there is an emphasis on local produce, and even in the national supermarket chains, such as Manor and Migros, there are variations in the cheese, wine, fruit and vegetable produce available from store to store in the different regions. Watches and chocolate will be on everyone's list of famous Swiss products but there are lots of other items that make great souvenirs and presents.

Watches and Jewellery

Switzerland is the world's largest watch manufacturer and there are scores of brand names and styles to choose from. Many shops specialise in just one or two brands but in the big cities you will find shops such as Les Ambassadeurs *(see page 74)* that stock a wide range. Switzerland is serious about maintaining its position as the world's leading watchmaker and in most shops you will find well-trained and knowledgeable staff. Much of the jewellery on sale in family-run shops is also of a high standard (and price). Some of the best materials and artisans are sourced from all over the world.

Traditional Goods and Crafts

There is a wide range of traditional craft goods apart from cuckoo clocks and alpine horns. Look out for wood carving (especially around Brienz), basketry, pottery, and also porcelain. Bopla is a manufacturer of Swiss china – its designs, utilising bold colours and exotic themes, are distinctive and eye-catching. Cotton, lace and embroidery are also of good quality – look out for these items in the northeast, in the St Gallen region, which is the traditional home of the Swiss textile industry. Fun items include cowbells and braces adorned with traditional Swiss motifs.

The Swiss army knife is a classic of Swiss design and is now well over 100 years old. These knives come in all sorts of sizes and variations – Victorinox is the brand name to look out for. In addition to individual shops and craft outlets, the nationwide chain of Heimatwerk shops (also at international airports) offers an excellent range of top-quality Swiss products.

Food and Wine

The great items to take home are of course cheese and chocolate – the most famous names in the latter category being Lindt, Suchard and Nestlé. The harder cheeses, such as Gruyères and Emmental, are the best to transport, and you will find regional cheeses, for example Pilatus on the market stalls of Lucerne, that you won't get back home. Swiss wines, with their nifty screw-cap tops, make an unusual present.

Prices

Electrical goods and food are generally quite cheap by European standards, but clothing, books, handicrafts and art will be expensive for many visitors.

The retail price of many goods includes 7.6 percent value-added tax. This sum can be reclaimed by foreign visitors making

Left: flower stall, Marktplatz, Basel
Right: a famous name in chocolate

purchases of over CHF400 by filling in a form available at the shop. Refunds can be claimed by post or at Geneva and Zürich airports.

Some cities operate guest card schemes that offer discounts at designated shops and restaurants and also on public transport *(see page 89)*.

City Shopping

Geneva

Geneva's main shopping district is on the left bank of the lake. The winding lanes and roads of the old town are lined with small art and antiques galleries and shops selling anything and everything from up-market kitchenware to children's toys. The Rue du Rhône and the Rue du Marché–Rue de la Croix d'Or–Rue de Rive at the foot of the old town, run parallel to the English Garden, and have a range of larger shops and department stores such as Globus (which has an excellent food hall at its Place du Molard entrance). Elm Books, an English-language bookshop, is located near here at Rue Versonnex 5.

If you want to buy a Swiss watch, the Rue du Rhône is the street to head for; a number of shops there sell a good range of makes – Les Ambassadeurs, at No 39, stocks one of the widest ranges. Carouge, a southern district of Geneva, is a great place for more low-key bric-à-brac browsing and bargain -hunting. Le Comptoir des Délices, Rue Saint-Victor 10, Carouge, is a wonderful delicatessen, and Prunelle, Place du Marché 3, is good for women's clothes.

Above: a big cheese
Right: there's no shortage of watch shops

Bern

The arcaded old town of Bern is the city's central shopping district, with Kramgasse and Marktgasse at its centre. The medieval arcades, which make an interesting and weatherproof place to shop, have a quite irresistible selection of small shops and cafés as well as department stores and galleries. Kramgasse is particularly good for antiques. Hein Posamenter at Münstergasse 33 sells a fabulous array of ribbons, some with Swiss motifs. Markthalle at Bubenbergplatz 9 (next to the station) is a delicatessen carrying a wide range of local and not so local foods. Arts and crafts emporia are plentiful in Kramgasse (try Heimatwerk at No 61). If you have a sweet tooth, head for Confiserie Eichenberger at Bahnhofplatz 5 or Confiserie Tschirren, Kramgasse 73, for a taste of local confectionery. If it's a Swiss army knife you're after, Messer Klötzli, at Rathausgasse 84, is probably your best bet. Ryfflihof, on Aarbergergasse–Neuengasse, is the city's leading department store.

Basel

Freie Strasse in the old town is a major shopping street and the roads running off it have interesting shops and galleries. The Globus and Epa AG department stores are on Marktplatz and Gerbergasse respectively.

Läckerli-huus, at Gerbergasse 57 and Greifengasse 2, is a tempting stop for confectionery, especially Basler Leckerli, which is manufactured to a traditional recipe. Schweizer Heimatwerk, Schneidergasse 2, and Füglistaller, Freie Strasse 23, are good for a range of high-quality Swiss products.

Zürich

The city of Zürich is a shopper's paradise and, although the reputation of its most famous street – Bahnhofstrasse – is one of ultra expensive and exclusive establishments, there are plenty of interesting stores with affordable prices. Bahnhofstrasse tends to get more exclusive the further south towards the lake you go – its northern end and the roads around it contain a number of chain department stores such as Jelmoli and Manor. Orell Füssli's The Bookshop at Bahnhofstrasse 70 is a large, exclusively English-language bookshop selling a wide range of fiction and non-fiction, including current bestsellers. Sprüngli has a number of tempting outlets including Bahnhofstrasse 67 and Löwenplatz 49. Schweizer Heimatwerk shops can be found at Rudolf Brun-Brücke, and there's a gallery-style shop at Rennweg 14. On the other side of the Limmat River, the old town has numerous small streets and winding alleys with a range of specialist boutiques, galleries and shops. Rindermarkt and Neumarkt are good for books and antiques – and hat shops. There's a travel book shop at Rindermarkt 20. Below the cathedral the range of interesting establishments continues – a cross-section of emporia includes Little Tibet at Kirchgasse 3 for Himalayan handicrafts, Kitch'n'Cook at Schifflände 32, with an array of designer kitchenware and gadgets, and the old-fashioned Schuh Haus Wilh Grab shoe shop on Kirchgasse.

MARKETS

While in Switzerland, you should definitely visit a fresh produce market. Most towns and cities have weekly markets – usually on a Saturday morning, and sometimes on a midweek morning too. They generally start early and wind down by early afternoon. Apart from a wide array of fresh fruit and vegetables there are usually bread, cheese and wine stalls selling local delicacies. They are a great place to pick up picnic items and snacks and, for a taste of Switzerland, to take home with you at the end of your visit. The following markets are some of the best:

Geneva – flea market in Plainpalais, open Wednesday and Saturday; crafts market in Place de la Fusterie, open Thursday; fresh produce market in Carouge, open Wednesday and Saturday.

Bern – fresh produce and craft market in Bundesplatz–Bärenplatz, open Tuesday and Saturday morning throughout the year and every day between May and October; handicrafts market in Münsterplatz open first Saturday of the month.

Basel – fresh produce market in Marktplatz every morning; new goods market in Barfüsserplatz, open Thursday mornings; flea market in Petersplatz every Saturday morning.

Zürich – fresh produce on Tuesday and Friday in Stadthausanlage; craft market in Rosenhof open Thursday and Saturday.

Above: a market stall in Ascona

EATING OUT

Swiss cuisine certainly does not conform to the popular stereotypes. Although of course you will find fondues and *rösti* on many menus, you will also find a lot else besides. There is, generally speaking, considerable care taken in the selection and preparation of high-quality fresh produce and also in the presentation of dishes. In the towns and cities many Swiss people eat out frequently – sometimes twice a day – and restaurants, many of which have been in operation for decades, concentrate on providing good, consistently high-quality meals, albeit at what may appear rather high prices.

Restaurants come in all types and sizes, and you can dine well in anything from a Co-op supermarket café to a Michelin-rated establishment. Even in the winter, many places, especially the ski resorts, get a lot of sunshine and you will find restaurants throughout the country that will serve meals on a heated terrace. Look out for some of the local names – *gasthof* and *gasthaus* in German-speaking Switzerland, *auberge* in the east and *osteria* and *grotto* in the Ticino.

If you have a car try heading out of town to a nearby village – even the smallest hamlet usually has a café or restaurant or two. Cable cars and funicular railways abound in the mountainous regions. Almost without exception at the main stops and at the summit you'll find a restaurant – even if you're not skiing or hiking these can be great lunch spots – and the views are free.

Swiss Cuisine

There is a good variety of cooking styles to be found throughout the country and throughout the seasons, with asparagus, local salads such as dandelion leaves *(dents de lion)*, wild mushrooms, wild game *(chasse)* and certain cheeses all making seasonal appearances.

Some of the well-known dishes, such as fondue, *raclette* (a block of melting cheese spread on boiled potatoes or bread) and *rösti* (fried grated potato) should definitely be sampled. You might want to accompany a fondue with white wine or black tea to aid digestion. Hot rich fondues are particularly

Above: the Swiss love terrace dining
Left: Valais wine

good after a day's skiing or hiking; you can find variations on the plain cheese version, including tomato or mushroom. If you order a *fondue bourguignonne* you'll be given-cubes of meat that you cook by dipping them into hot oil, and if you opt for *fondue chinoise* thinly sliced beef which is dipped into a hot spicy stock.

Regional specialities include lake fish such as perch, trout and char in the west of the country around Geneva and Neuchâtel; air-dried beef *(walliserfleisch)* in the Valais; smoked sausage *(wurst)* dishes and also wonderful breads *(brot)* in the German-speaking part of Switzerland around Bern, Lucerne and Zürich; and salamis, risottos, minestrone and polenta dishes in the Ticino. *Cazzöla* – a sausage, cabbage and potato stew – is a local favourite here.

For vegetarians many restaurants will have pasta dishes and omelettes on offer but a mixed salad can also work well as a main course. Most restaurants normally have a good, if limited, range of puddings with *tortes* featuring strongly in central and northern regions, and delicious Italian-style ice cream and sorbets in the south. There are lots of regional sweet specialities such as *Zuger kirschtorte*, a rich kirsch-flavoured almond cake, found in the Lucerne region, *Leckerli* in Basel and the marzipan-filled *Bärli-Biber* in Appenzell.

Wines

Little Swiss wine is exported, so sampling the local specialities means discovering some new tastes for many visitors. The Valais is the country's top wine-producing region with its surprisingly hearty Dôle, light Oeil de Perdrix (rosé) and crisp Fendant (white).

The shores of Lake Geneva and Lake Neuchâtel produce some interesting whites, notably Dézaley and Chasselas. Ticino, in the sunnier south, produces some rich reds, including Merlot and Nostrano. A couple of the country's liqueurs are *kirsch*, produced near Zug, and *ratafià*, a walnut liqueur from the Ticino.

Eating Hours

Meal times are considered sacrosanct, with lunch usually being taken between noon and 1pm and evening meals often finished by 9pm. In the cities and main towns you will find that eateries stay open until late, but in smaller towns and villages in the country it can be difficult to find restaurants willing to accept customers after 9pm. Many establishments close one day a week and also for an annual holiday – always check opening times beforehand.

Budget Ideas

Eating out is a comparatively expensive activity but there are ways to minimise the cost. For example, you can ask the waiter for local decanted wines by amount (decilitres – *'décis'*) rather than ordering a bottle; and at lunchtime, the cheapest option is to go for the *plat du jour* or *tagesteller*.

Larger establishments will often have two separate dining areas – a café serving a relatively limited menu, and a more expensive (and more formal) restaurant. If you're watching your budget and are not overly concerned about ambience, many Migros supermarkets have good-value restaurants, and the countrywide chains Mövenpick and Manora are also reasonable.

Key to Prices

$ = up to CHF50
$$ = – CHF50–100
$$$ = over CHF100
These prices are based on a two- or three-course meal with a glass of wine.

Above: Mövenpick eateries are popular with locals and visitors alike

Western Switzerland

Coppet

Hôtel du Lac
Grand Rue
Tel: 022-776 1521
Coppet is 10 minutes by local train from Gare Cornavin or in summer by lake steamer. The Hôtel du Lac has a terrace overlooking the lake. Try the lake fish – *filets de perche*. $$

Geneva

Au Pied de Cochon
Place Bourg de Four 4
Tel: 022-310 4797
Bustling bistro in the old town's main square. Its rich and varied French menu includes pigs' trotters. $$

La Grignotière
Hôtel Noga Hilton
19 Quai du Mont-Blanc
Tel: 022-908 9086
Terrace restaurant overlooking the lake and the Jet d'Eau. Specialises in good quality international cuisine. $$$

Le Palais de Justice
8 Place du Bourg-de-Four
Tel: 022-318 3737
A modest eatery in the heart of the old town with a good range of dishes. $

Gruyères

Hôtel de Ville
Tel: 026-921 2424
This fine establishment on the main street serves a range of local dishes. It has a good terrace for summer dining. $$

Montreux

Hostellerie du Lac
Rue de Quai 12
Tel: 021-963 3271
Has a great location, with terrace on the lakeside. It's a lively spot on summer evenings and serves traditional Swiss dishes. $$

Le Museum Restaurant
Rue de la Gare 40
Tel: 021-963 1662
Just behind the station, this restaurant, linked to the museum, is housed in a traditional cellar and serves a variety of local food including *raclette*, lake fish, and meat dishes. Closed Sun and Mon. $$

Neuchâtel

Le Banneret
Rue Fleury 1
Tel: 032-725 2861
Situated in the old town, this attractive restaurant with a small terrace serves great pasta. Closed Sun. $$

Nyon

La Croix-Verte
Rue Perdtemps 7
Tel: 022-361 1539
A cosy Italian restaurant serving pizzas, pasta dishes and other fare. It has a large garden terrace that is open in the summer. $$

Sierre

La Poste
Rue du Bourg 22
Tel: 027-455 1003
Typically Valaisan, with lots of local dishes and wines. $

Sion

Restaurant l'Enclos de Valère
Rue des Châteaux 18
Tel: 027-323 3230
Good for lunch – the garden terrace is very pleasant in summer. French food. $$

Verbier

Le Rosalp
Rue de Médran
Tel: 027-771 6323
This top hotel has a restaurant, brasserie and bar – all serving fabulous food – presided over by one of Switzerland's top chefs, Roland Pierroz. The Bar du Rosalp offers the best Valais wines. Booking advised. $$$

Zermatt

Grill Restaurant Spycher
Hotel Aristella
Tel: 027-967 1141
This chalet-style restaurant serves a wide range of dishes and has an extensive wine list. Good for après-ski coffee liqueurs. $$

Central Switzerland

Basel

Fischrestaurant, Café Spitz
Rheingasse/Greifengasse 2
Tel: 061-685 1111
A fine old building with a nice terrace, on the eastern end of Mittlerebrücke. Specialises in freshwater fish and seafood. $$

Zur Mägd Wirtshaus
St Johanns-Vorstadt 29
Tel: 061-322 0502
An old guildhall, decorated in traditional style, which serves lots of local specialities. North of the old town, near Johanniterbrücke. Closed Sun, Jul–Sep. $$

Left: a good option in Interlaken
Right: blending formality and style

Bern

Ratskeller
Gerechtigkeitsgasse 81
Tel: 031-311 1771
A long-established restaurant with *keller*, in the old town. The menu includes interesting meat and fish dishes. $$

Zum Äusseren Stand
Zeughausgasse 17
Tel: 031-311 3205
This fine establishment, behind the Kornhaus, excels at fish and seafood. Both sea- and freshwater-fish dishes are served. $$$

Brienz (for Ballenberg)

Restaurant Steinbock
Hauptstrasse 123
Tel: 033-951 4055
Always busy, this restaurant serves good local lake fish dishes. $$

Interlaken

Gasthof Hirschen
Haupstrasse 11
Tel: 033-822 1545
A typically Swiss chalet dating back to the 16th century. A wide choice of top-quality cuisine is served in a cosy setting. $$

Lucerne

Restaurant zur Laterne
Reussteg 9
Tel: 041-240 2543
On the south bank, close to Reussbrücke, this pleasantly old-fashioned restaurant offers an extensive and reasonably priced menu. $$

Zunfthaus zu Pfistern
Kornmarkt 4
Tel: 041-410 3650
This traditional-style restaurant, complete with old-fashioned gas lighting, serves equally traditional cuisine and is located conveniently right in the centre of the old town. $$

Thun

Walliser Kanne
Marktgasse 3
Tel: 033-222 9414
Traditional dishes, including fondue, are the order of the day at this small, friendly and central spot. $

Weggis

Hotel Gotthard-Schönau am See
Gotthardstrasse 11
Tel: 041-390 2114
In the summer months, the hotel terrace overlooking the lake is an exceptionally pleasant spot in which to lunch or dine. The restaurant is modest but it serves a good range of cuisine, including pizzas. $

Eastern Switzerland

Appenzell

Gasthaus Linde Appenzell
off Landsgemeindeplatz
Tel: 071-787 1376
A traditional wood-panelled Appenzell restaurant serving a mixture of good-value traditional and international cuisine, and local beers. $

Bellinzona

Castelgrande Grotto San Michele
Tel: 091-826 2353
The grotto terrace restaurant is the cheaper of the two in the Castelgrande. It offers great food, views and estate wines. $$

Chur

Obelisco
Vazerolgasse 12
Tel: 081-252 5858
Lovely Italian restaurant located in the heart of the old town and serving a wide range of dishes, including pizzas and pasta. It also offers a pleasant terrace for eating out in summer. $$

Locarno

Carcani-Mövenpick
Piazza G Motta
Ascona
Tel: 091-785 1717
This atmospheric eatery is part of the good-value nationwide Mövenpick chain. It offers a wide choice of dishes and a great location right on the lake. $$

Costa Azzurra
Via Bastoria 13
Locarno-Solduna
Tel: 091-751 3802
This traditional grotto 20 minutes walk from the old town serves a splendid selection of fish and meat dishes. There's a cosy restaurant and a shady riverside terrace. $$

Lugano

Cantinone
Piazza Cioccaro
Tel: 091-923 1068
Near the cathedral, on the corner of the *piazza*, Cantinone serves an extensive range of delicious pizzas and pastas. $.

Above: former guildhalls have been transformed into restaurants in Zürich
Right: try St Gallen's Zum Goldenen Schäfli for its menu and atmosphere

St Gallen

Zum Goldenen Schäfli
Metzgergasse 7
Tel: 071-223 3737
Situated in a 17th-century guildhall, Zum Goldenen Schäfli has lots of local character and an appealing menu. Try the famous local *bratwurst*. $$

St Moritz

Veltlinerkeller
Via del Bagn 11
Tel: 081-833 4009
Veltlinerkeller is one of St Moritz's favourite eating establishments. Prices aren't too high and there's a good choice of dishes, including fish. $$

Schaffhausen

Fischerzunft
Rheinquai 8
Tel: 052-625 3281
This is one of Switzerland's top restaurants and prices match the accolade. However, the food is wonderful, especially the fish dishes, and the riverside setting is decidedly memorable. $$$

Scuol

Hotel Traube
Stradun
Tel: 081-861 0700
The restaurant of this modest hotel includes a rooftop terrace and offers a delightful range of excellent good-value dishes. Try the local *grappa*. $$

Stein am Rhein

Sonne
Rathausplatz 127
Tel: 052-741 2128
Sonne is one of Stein am Rhein's most famous establishments – culinary or otherwise. The café, below the more expensive small restaurant, offers delicious cuisine at reasonable prices. $$

Zürich

Haus zum Rüden
1st floor
Limmatquai 42
Tel: 01-261 9566
Haus zum Rüden is an marvellous 13th-century guildhall that offers excellent food in truly magnificent surroundings. Closed Sat and Sun. $$$

Hilti
Sihlstrasse 28
Tel: 01-227 7000
Just off Bahnhofstrasse, this is one of the oldest vegetarian restaurants in Europe. The buffet option is especially good value for money. $$

Zic Zac Rock Garden
Marktgasse 17
Tel: 01-261 2191
Located in the heart of the old town, the Zic Zac Rock Garden and its music attract a young, trendy crowd. It is particularly appealing if you like good old-fashioned hamburgers. $

ENTERTAINMENT AND ACTIVITIES

There's a lot going on in both the cities and the countryside in Switzerland, though much of it is on a fairly small scale and you might have to work at uncovering it. Apart from in the major cities there is little in the way of traditional nightlife, except in the ski resorts, which all have a number of cosy après-ski drinking and dining establishments, and even the smallest villages will have one or two café/bars where you can relax over a glass of the local wine.

There are flourishing music scenes – jazz (in the cities) and classical in particular. Most sizeable towns and cities have festivals in summer, notably Montreux, Nyon, Verbier, Bern, Schaffhausen and Gstaad. Bellinzona stages open-air opera in Castelgrande in late July–early August and a number of cities have open-air cinemas in July and August. These include Geneva, Lausanne and Basel, and Locarno which also hosts an International Film Festival in early August.

Switzerland has a number of spa towns; some of the modern complexes are very extensive. A day out at a spa resort can be relaxing, especially after a number of days skiing or walking on the slopes. The major spa towns include Scuol in the Engadine Valley, Yverdon-les-Bains which is between Lausanne and Neuchâtel, and Baden 20km (12 miles) north of Zürich.

Activities

If you're keen on outdoor activities you will find a huge range in Switzerland, complete with some of the best facilities in the world. Skiing, snowboarding and numerous other winter sports are the attractions that draw enormous numbers of foreign visitors to the country. The large number of resorts cater to all requirements. The sheer beauty of the natural environment has long drawn hikers and mountaineers and today there is a vast and well-maintained network of hiking and mountain-biking trails, both long and short. Given the numerous lakes, it's not surprising that sailing and water sports in general are also extremely popular in the summer.

Skiing

Ski resorts in Switzerland range from the large ones such as Verbier, with its plethora of pistes and facilities, to individual cross-country trails high in the Jura. It is usually possible to hire any equipment you will need at most locations. You will find some flood-lit cross-country trails for evening skiing – which can be magical. There are a few resorts where you can ski all year round, but generally the season is from late December to early April.

Snowboarding is extremely popular, and there are other snow sports, such as bob-sledding, mono-skiing and heli-skiing. Tobogganing – a particularly good idea if you're skiing with children – is also widely catered for at resorts. The following resorts are all at, or close to, destinations described in this guide.

Jura – the small resorts throughout the Jura are within an hour's drive of Geneva and Neuchâtel and are very popular with the local Swiss and the French. Particularly good for cross-country skiing. Two of the main resorts are St Cergue and Lac de Jeux. Quiet and family oriented.

Moléson-sur Gruyères – small purpose-built chalet village with both downhill and cross-country skiing. Good for beginners.

Verbier – a large, busy resort in the Valais with an extensive range of slopes but few for the beginner. It's particularly popular with British skiers. A lively après-ski scene.

Zermatt – a long-established chalet town, car-free and with extensive facilities and medium to hard slopes. Year-round skiing is possible on the glacier. It has an abundance of attractions, and classic views when you want a break from the activity.

Mürren – a delightful car-free small village resort with lots of facilities and slopes and a long tradition of winter sports – all in the most scenic of locations.

Grindelwald – a large, modern chalet village spread over a wide valley floor. There are slopes and off-piste areas for all abilities, especially beginners. Particularly good resort for children.

Mt Kronberg – off the beaten track and away from the big crowds, but there is only limited downhill and cross-country in quiet, scenic surroundings.

St Moritz – the priciest and glitziest of all the resorts. The skiing is excellent, with a range of good facilities and slopes. Lots of expensive diversions by way of shops and nightlife.

Lower Engadine – the towns and villages located in the far east of the country offer some of the quietest, most traditional skiing holidays. Some downhill and lots of cross-country on offer.

Hiking

Switzerland has tens of thousands of kilometres of marked hiking trails covering the gamut from one-hour walks to week-long hikes. They are clearly signposted with yellow markers and usually give an idea of how long it takes to reach a particular destination. Alpine routes are marked in red and white; the highest trails, marked in blue, are strictly for the fittest and most experienced and should only be attempted with a guide. You'll find routes from virtually everywhere including cities. Almost all cable car and funicular stations have a choice of walks from the top. The well-maintained trails regularly pass through villages and near wayside *buvettes* (simple cafés) for refreshments, but do always take plenty of water.

Local tourist offices can always help with suggestions, maps and finding guides. There are long-distance footpaths, for example up some of the passes, that follow traditional trade and pilgrimage routes. Along these you should find mountain refuge huts for overnight stays. Get details of these routes and other information from the Swiss Alpine Club, tel: 031-370 1818, fax: 031-370 1800, www.sac-cas.ch and the Swiss Hiking Federation, tel: 061-606 9340, fax: 061-606 9345, www.swisshiking.ch.

Other Outdoor Activities

Other sports and activities include sailing and windsurfing. Many of Switzerland's lakes have small, south-facing beaches for sunbathing. Cycling and mountain biking are popular. Renting mountain bikes is easy – you can usually find a route down from a railway station if the ride uphill is too tough. Local tourist offices will provide on-the-spot details. River rafting is popular in some areas, especially along stretches of the Rhine near Chur. Ballooning, horse riding and skating are among other popular activities.

Left: relaxing at a spa
Above: let loose on Verbier's slopes

CALENDAR OF EVENTS

Switzerland is a popular destination throughout the year with lots of events and festivals to entertain visitors. In addition to internationally renowned attractions such as the Montreux Jazz Festival, there are hundreds of local fairs and festivities in towns and villages across the country.

For all the relevant details of particular events, contact either local tourist offices in Switzerland, or alternatively the Switzerland Travel Centre in London tel: 0800-00 200 30.

To be assured of getting tickets and also accommodation for the three most illustrious international events, it is advisable to book well ahead.

- Montreux Jazz Festival (mid-July) www.montreuxjazz.com
- Nyon Paléo (late July) www.paleo.ch
- Locarno Film Festival (early August) www.pardo.ch

January

The *Schlitteda*, a procession of horse-drawn sleighs with costumed riders, that takes place in St Moritz.

January, February and March are the three main skiing months in Switzerland.

February

The very popular *Marathon des Neiges Franco-Suisses* cross-country race takes place in the La Chaux-de-Fonds region in mid-February.

March

The *Chalandamarz* is a traditional spring custom, held on March 1 in the Engadine Valley, where young people parade, ringing cowbells to chase winter away.

Throughout the first three weeks in March *spring carnivals* take place in numerous towns and villages, including Geneva, La Chaux-de-Fonds, Lucerne, Zug, Bern, Basel, Zürich, St Gallen, Chur, the Engadine Valley and Bellinzona. Each lasts a couple of days or so and often includes masked parades.

The Palexpo exhibition halls are the venue for the huge *Geneva International Motor Show* in early March.

April

Open-air public 'parliaments' or *Landsgemeinde* take place at the end of April and the beginning of May in towns throughout Appenzellerland – Appenzell, Glarus and Trogen.

Early in the month Locarno, with its wonderfully mild climate, puts on the *Camellia Flower Festival.*

May

Early on during the month Montreux stages the *Golden Rose International Television Festival.*

June

Open-air performances of Schiller's *Wilhelm Tell* are staged in German in Interlaken, from late June to early September.

Above: a break for refreshments during a cattle festival

The *Bol d'Or* sailing regatta is a big, colourful race on Lake Geneva in mid-June.

July

In the middle two weeks of July the world-class *International Montreux Jazz Festival* attracts a strong line-up of artists and a big audience.

Nyon's *Paléo* music festival focuses on international rock and folk music. It's like a smaller version of Glastonbury – usually without the mud.

From mid-July to mid-August *classical music concerts* are staged in a number of villages in the Engadine Valley.

August

The entire country celebrates *Swiss National Day* on August 1 with parades, bonfires and fireworks.

Geneva's *Fêtes de Genève* take place in early August when the city is most definitely in holiday mood. Celebrations incorporate impressive firework displays, colourful parades and numerous open-air concerts.

The increasingly important *Locarno International Film Festival* takes place in early August with open-air screenings in the city's Piazza Grande.

Bern is also in festival mode in August, when *Bern's Old Town Festival* features a diverse array of concerts and events.

The dramatic setting of Castelgrande in Bellinzona is used to stage *open-air opera* during the last week in August.

September

Early in September Bellinzona's traditional *wine festival* is celebrated.

In late September and early October *Brächete* festivals (celebrating the process of turning flax into linen) take place in Langnau and the Ballenberg Open-Air Museum.

October

Early October (but sometimes also in late September, depending on the weather and the region) sees the classic spectacle of *désalpes*, when cattle descend from their highland pastures – all decked out in ribbons and flowers for their journey. This can be witnessed in various locations but try the Jura villages and those around Lucerne.

Right: at a Rilke book festival

November

Bern's 600-year-old *Zibelemärit* or Onion Market takes place on the fourth Monday in the month when the city centre is awash with onion stalls.

The early November *Kermis (Autumn Fair)* in Basel is the largest in Switzerland and is the oldest continuously held fair in the country.

December

On 11 December Geneva's *Fête de l'Escalade* celebrates the successful defence of the city in 1602 against the Duke of Savoy, whose troops attempted to scale *(escalader)* the city walls. One soldier was famously drenched in boiling soup before having the soup cauldron smashed over his head, by way of repulsion. In commemoration of this, chocolate cauldrons are produced today and ritually smashed and eaten. Torchlit processions in period costume, a bonfire in the cathedral square and a public run through the old town round off the festivities.

Illuminated boats are floated down the Limmat River in Zürich during *Lichterschwimmen*, which takes place during the third week in December.

Christmas markets are held in a number of towns – including Lucerne, Montreux and Basel – throughout the month.

TI-1607

Practical *Information*

GETTING THERE

By Air

Switzerland has several international airports even though it is a small country. The principal ones are Zürich and Geneva, but there are also international flights to Basel, Bern and Lugano. It is hard to find very cheap fares to Swiss cities, partly because there is so much business travel. But the advent of Go and MyTravelLite flights from London, Liverpool and Birmingham has been responsible for introducing more cheap fares.

British Airways (tel: 0845-773 3377, www.ba.com) and Swiss (tel: 0845-601 0956, www.swiss.com) are the main carriers from Heathrow, Gatwick, and London City airports in London. There are also direct flights from Birmingham, Manchester and Edinburgh. In winter there is a weekly Crossair flight from Heathrow to Sion, which is close to many of the skiing resorts in the Valais.

If you're flying to Geneva, Zürich or Basel and continuing on to your destination by public transport, you can take advantage of the Fly-Rail Baggage service. For under £10 per item, your luggage will be delivered to the train station nearest your accommodation. Once you check your bags in, you don't see them again until you arrive.

If you're coming from the US, try one of the following:

- Airhitch, 2641 Broadway, New York, NY 10025 (tel: 1-800-326 2009 or 212-864 2000; www.airhitch.org)
- Skylink, 265 Madison Ave, 5th Fl, New York, NY 10016 (tel: 212-599 0430)
- STA Travel, 5900 Wilshire Blvd, Suite 2110, LosAngeles, CA 90036 (tel: 1-800-777 0112; www.sta-travel.com)

By Train

The traditional way to travel to Switzerland is by train. Assuming that you have the time, the leisurely scenic journey can be part of the holiday. The quickest option is to go by the Eurostar train via the Channel Tunnel to Paris (3 hrs) and then change trains (and stations), and take the TGV to Geneva (3 hrs 40 mins) or Zürich (6 hours). Eurostar arrives at the Gare du Nord in Paris, TGV services leave from the Gare de Lyon, so a trip across the city is required. There are slower services to Basel, Zürich and Chur from the Gare de l'Est, which is very close to the Gare du Nord. Swiss Federal Railways (tel: 0900-300 300, www.rail.ch) can provide details of the timetable and fare options.

By Car

It is possible to drive from southeast England to Switzerland in a day, though it is a very long day behind the wheel. To visit western Switzerland, the route from Calais is the most direct, and it is almost all motorway. Make sure your insurance cover is adequate and note that you will need to buy a CHF40 motorway sticker *(vignette)* at the border to use Swiss motorways. You must carry a driving licence and vehicle registration document. For vehicles over 3.5 tons you must pay tax at the border. You are obliged to display your nationality sticker on the car and to carry a warning triangle.

TRAVEL ESSENTIALS

Passports and Visas

A valid passport should be carried at all times. EU nationals don't need visas.

Left: the lakeside at Ascona
Right: for a leisurely journey

Health

No vaccinations or inoculations are required for visitors from Europe and North America. Switzerland has a private medical system but it is expensive. You should take out adequate medical insurance cover in advance.

Seasons and When to Visit

High season is July–August, Christmas, New Year and February–mid-March. Accommodation prices are usually much higher then and availability in some resorts is limited. But you can enjoy Switzerland's natural beauty, attractive old towns, high-quality activities and local festivals at any time of the year. Obviously winters are cold, and travel can be limited at higher altitudes, especialy through certain passes in the Alps. Summers are quite hot, particularly south of the Alps. The country's infrastructure and

tourist sector is excellent at coping with weather extremes. In the mountain resorts, November and May tend to be so quiet that many hotels and eateries temporarily close.

Clothing

Whatever the time of year, you should bring waterproofs and some warm clothes. Good walking shoes are essential if you are planning to do some hiking. On summer evenings long-sleeved garments will help protect you from marauding midges and mosquitoes near lakesides. The Swiss generally adopt a decidedly casual approach to clothing styles in all but the most expensive restaurants.

Customs

The import of currency into the country is unrestricted. Tourists can bring up to 2 litres of wine and 1 litre of spirits and up to 200 cigarettes. Gifts up to CHF100 in value are allowed free of duty. Largely due to the lower price of goods in France and Italy, there are occasional spot searches at customs posts.

GETTING ACQUAINTED

Electricity

The current is 220 volts and plugs are continental, so an adaptor can be useful.

Time

Swiss time is one hour ahead of GMT.

Geography

Switzerland has a varied topography but is, of course, characterised by its Alpine massifs. The Jura mountains in the north run east–west from Basel to Geneva. The strip between the Jura and the Alps – the Mittelland – consists of rolling plains and hills and crystal-clear lakes. From here the Alps rise up and cover the entire east–west breadth of the country, dotting the skyline with peaks such as the Matterhorn, Jungfrau and Eiger. There are numerous passes through the Alps into France, Italy and Austria. Ticino, in the foothills of the Alps, shares the lakes of northern Italy and basks in a noticeably warmer Mediterranean climate.

Government and Economy

Politically, the tendency is to right-wing governments, but most major issues are settled by referenda, which give the people a democratic say in important matters and policy changes. The country's federal system of government gives considerable power to the individual cantons.

Most Swiss residents enjoy a high standard of living, and unemployment rates are low. The financial and insurance sector, tourism, engineering, pharmaceuticals, new technologies and agriculture are the key employers. The farming industry and public transport, considered vital for economic and environmental reasons, are subsidised. The country enjoys an unusual position within

Above: the historic uniform of Swiss soldiers modelled by a modern non-belligerent

Europe and the world – it's not a member of the EU and is home to many international agencies and UN organisations. Some 25 percent of the workforce is non-Swiss.

Etiquette

Generally the Swiss are polite and helpful. Privacy is respected, which can be interpreted as a lack of friendliness. This apparent coldness is compensated by the traditional Swiss greeting – three kisses on the cheek, though a handshake is the norm on a first meeting. Almost all conversations – in shops and post offices, with ticket collectors and passing walkers – start with a greeting, and foreigners' attempts to speak the local language are always appreciated.

Money Matters

Swiss francs are officially represented as CHF but you will see other abbreviations such as SFr. Any amount of foreign currency and travellers' cheques can be brought into the country. Swiss bankers travellers' cheques can be bought in the UK and used for paying bills in hotels, restaurants and shops. All major credit cards are widely accepted and ATMs can be found almost everywhere; there is usually an option for instructions to be displayed in English.

Tipping

Generally, service charges are included in hotel, restaurant and taxi prices but it is quite common to leave a small additional amount for excellent service in restaurants.

GETTING AROUND

By Train

Switzerland's railways – the Swiss Federal Railway (SBB-CFF-FFS) – have a deserved reputation for speed and efficiency. The network is extensive and you can get to the smallest mountain resorts quite easily. If you are planning to travel around by train Swiss Federal Railways issues a 'Swiss Pass' that gives unlimited travel on trains, ferries and most mountain-post buses. These passes make travel costs surprisingly moderate for a country with the reputation of being expensive. Tickets can be bought for different periods – 4, 8, 15, 22 days or a month, and you need make only one or two long trips for them to represent a major saving on the cost of individual tickets. If two or more adults travel together the prices are reduced by 15 percent. The Swiss Pass also entitles you to a reduction on the price of most privately owned funicular railways.

Other money-saving tickets include:

- the Swiss Flexi Pass for unlimited travel on specified days within a one-month period
- the Swiss Transfer Ticket which, for a fixed price, allows travel from a frontier railway station or airport to a single destination and back (particularly useful for skiing holidays)
- the Swiss Half-Fare card which gives a 50 percent discount on any number of train tickets for an individual for one month.

Enquiries regarding the Swiss Transfer Ticket should be made in advance at the Switzerland Travel Centre in London. You can obtain a train timetable (which includes buses, mountain buses, cable cars, boats and ferries) from Swiss Federal Railways. Even if the transfer times appear tight you can almost always rely on the system to stick to the timetable.

While lots of train routes pass through spectacular scenery, a handful of routes have special excursion trains. A ride in one of these isn't about getting from A to B but is taken for sheer pleasure. Prices are generally much higher than for the scheduled service but, if your time is limited and your wallet isn't, the excursion can be a memorable experience. You usually have to reserve a place on these trips. Features can include panoramic carriages with glass roofs for unimpeded viewing. The Glacier Express connects St Moritz and Zermatt, the Golden

Right: a traditional form of transport

Pass Express Geneva and Lucerne, and the William Tell Express Lucerne and Lugano. The latter operates only in summer and starts with a boat trip across Lake Lucerne.

By Car

Travelling by car in Switzerland is generally straightforward. Motorways link all the major centres and even the most minor of mountain routes is well-maintained. A huge amount of freight is transported by train so there aren't too many heavy trucks on the roads. Traffic can be heavy in and around the cities but, compared with most Western urban conurbations, congestion is minimal.

Speed limits are 120kph (75mph) on motorways, 80 kph (50mph) on main roads outside built-up areas, and 50kph (30mph) in towns. Vehicles towing caravans or trailers are restricted to 80kph (50mph). The maximum caravan width is 2.5m (8.2ft) and 2.3m (7.5ft) on a few mountain roads. Green road signs indicate motorways, blue signs are for main roads. You will find a lot of self-service petrol stations, which accept payment by credit card.

Driving across the mountain passes is not as onerous as it might sound. There is always a restaurant and ample parking spaces at which you can stop and take in the view. Some passes stay open all year, others are closed from November to May. At the base of the pass road you will see a sign telling you whether the pass is open or not. At some passes you will have the option of taking the road or a motor rail service – the latter can be a good idea in bad weather or if you're carrying queasy passengers.

The big bookshops in the major cities have an extensive selection of road and hiking maps, and local shops and garages have a more limited and local range. All the tourist offices, large and small, will have maps of their area which vary in their detail and usability. The Landeskarte der Schweiz (Federal Topographical Office) produces very good up-to-date 1:50,000 and 1: 25,000 maps for hiking that are widely available in Switzerland and at specialist UK stores.

By Air

With such a fast, efficient and relatively cheap railway system, flying internally is an option rarely used by visitors. There are plenty of flights between the principal domestic airports – Zürich, Geneva, Bern, Basel and Lugano, but prices are very high. Crossair operates most of the internal flights.

By Boat and Ferry

The network of ferry and boat services around Switzerland's major lakes is fairly extensive during the summer (May–Oct), but very limited during the winter months. On many of the lakes, the boats and ferries are old paddle-steamers, most of which have restaurants. These can make for a very pleasant day or half-day excursion. The service is principally aimed at the leisure market, rather than offering fast links or commuter services. Swiss Pass tickets can be used on most of these services. If you're planning to travel by boat only, a Swiss Boat Pass gives a 50 percent reduction on ticket prices.

By Bus

The yellow 'postbus' (PTT) is an icon of Swiss life. It offers an extensive transport service to small, remote places. The PTTs are convenient to use and are covered by the Swiss Pass system. Timetables are very reliable and in most places there is seamless co-ordination between train arrivals and departures and the bus timetable.

Bus terminals are usually located in front of railway stations, and you can expect connections to be free of hassle. Villages and sights that are too small or remote to have a railway are serviced by the postbus. If you

Above: facing the future

want to walk without a heavy bag, a post-bus service of delivering unaccompanied baggage to a post office can be useful. There is a fee per item – ask at the post office if you want to use this facility.

Mountain Transport

The sheer variety and abundance of transport options in the mountains is staggering. Some of the larger resorts will have more than 100 individual routes providing a comprehensive network for skiing, hiking and sightseeing in the higher altitudes.

There are mountain railways, funiculars, cable-cars, gondolas, chairlifts and draglifts; on most, a discount is available with a Swiss Pass. Many of these services run to a timetable but some close in the quietest months (usually November and May) for servicing and repairs.

Transport in the Cities

All Swiss cities have an integrated transport network of buses, trolleybuses and trams. Zürich, being the biggest city, also has a network of commuter trains (S-Bahn). In most cases these services are included within the Swiss Pass system. If you don't have a Swiss Pass you can buy a day pass and, if you're travelling on a long-distance train, you can ask for a ticket that covers transport in the city as well.

If, however, you are planning to make just the occasional short journey, you will need to obtain a ticket from a machine at the bus stop. You can't buy tickets on board the vehicle – in Switzerland, you are expected to be honest. Potential fare-dodgers should be warned that ticket inspections are common and fines for travelling without a valid ticket are steep.

Cycling

Cycling, both in the cities and out in the countryside, is extremely popular. Given the terrain, cycling can require a level of fitness well beyond many of us, but if you are keen to use this ecologically friendly mode of transport, it is very easy to rent a bike. The major railway stations have cycle-hire outlets and you will come across plenty of other places from which to rent a bike in the cities and resorts.

Right: pointing the way for hikers

HOURS

Business hours are generally Mon–Fri 8am–noon and 2–5pm. Shop opening hours vary somewhat but tend to be Mon–Fri 9am–6.30pm, Sat 8am–6.30pm. On Thursdays many stores and supermarkets stay open until 8 or 9pm. Virtually all shops are closed on Sundays and public holidays, although for emergency items convenience shops at petrol stations may be open. Many of the smaller towns and villages have a day or half-day closing mid-week, and some smaller city centre shops may not open on Monday morning. Post offices usually close for lunch and are generally open only until 11am on Saturday. Some cafés and restaurants may close one or two days a week. Most museums are closed Monday.

Public Holidays

1 January – New Year's Day
Good Friday, Easter Sunday and Monday
Ascension Day – 40 days after Easter
Whit Sunday & Monday – 7 weeks after Easter
1 August – National Day
25, 26 December – Christmas, Boxing Day

ACCOMMODATION

Key to Prices

$ = up to CHF150
$$ = CHF150–300
$$$ = over CHF300
Prices are based on a double room with breakfast, including tax.

Types of Accommodation

The country has a long, hospitable tradition of welcoming visitors; many hostelries were established in the mid-19th century or even earlier. Hotels and self-catering chalets form the bulk of visitor accommodation options but there are other choices, including youth hostels, farm holidays, camping and spa

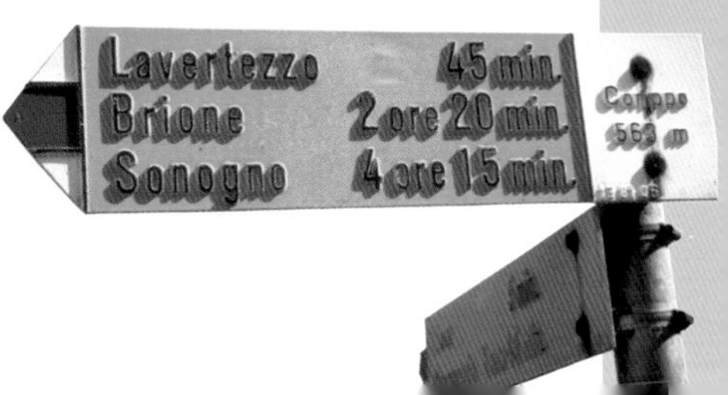

resorts. The Switzerland Travel Centre and local tourist offices can supply information about the whole range.

Airports and main railway stations have hotel reservation facilities but bear in mind that during peak season, or if there are major events or trade fairs going on in the main cities, choice will be limited. The vast number of hotels that are members of the Swiss Hotel Association are listed on the www.swisshotels.ch website.

Self-catering chalets are popular and usually well maintained. Camping is the cheapest option – the country has clean, well-run campsites in every town. Farm-stays and bed-and-breakfasts are also good options and are increasingly popular. Moreover, there's a scheme known as Sleeping in the Hay, by which farmers provide a (clean) barn in which you can sleep dormitory-style on the hay.

For a good choice of accommodation of any kind during the peak seasons, book well in advance. High winter season is Christmas and New Year and Feb–mid-March; summer is July–early September. November and May are generally low season; in some resorts hotels may be closed during these months.

Prices

Whatever the price category, you will find the standard of hotel rooms good, although at the lower end you may have to share a bathroom. Rates can be quoted per person or for the room so be sure you check this when making enquiries, and always ask if there is a discount if you're staying for more than three nights or visiting outside peak seasons. You may well be presented with a guest card – these entitle you to a discount at some of the local restaurants, sights, and on some local transport.

Western Switzerland

Coppet

Hôtel d'Orange
Grand Rue 61
Tel: 022-776 1037
Fax: 022-776 2540
This modest hotel (12 rooms) in the pretty village of Coppet is easily reached from Geneva (10 minutes by local train from Gare Cornavin). It's friendly, comfortable and a good budget option for stays in Geneva. There is a good restaurant in the basement. $.

Geneva

Hôtel Les Armures
1 Rue du Puits St Pierre
Tel: 022-310 9172
Fax: 022-310 9846
Small, attractive hotel situated in the heart of the old town. A favourite choice of visiting dignitaries. $$$

Hôtel Eden
Rue de Lausanne 135
Tel: 022-716 3700
Fax: 022-731 5260
A three-star hotel between the international district and the old town overlooking a park and the lake. Offers spacious rooms and parking. $$

Hôtel Luserna
12 Avenue de Luserna
Tel: 022-949 5656
Fax: 022-949 5636
A traditional villa with a large garden, this medium-sized hotel is well located for the station and international organisations. $

Gruyères

Hôtel de la Fleur-de-Lys
Tel: 026-921 2108
Fax: 026-921 3605
This small hotel is one of only four in Gruyères and is the cheapest. Rooms are simple and rustic. $$

Above: a good choice if you're looking for spacious rooms in Geneva

Montreux

Hôtel Righi
Glion
Tel: 021-966 1818
Fax: 021-961 1512
This grand belle époque hotel at Glion, a little way above Montreux, commands great views of the town and Alps; in a lovely quiet location with an attractive garden and terrace. $$

Du Pont
Rue du Pont 12
Tel/Fax: 021-963 2249
Located in the old town, away from the lake, this is a small, friendly hotel that serves wholesome food. $.

Neuchâtel

Hôtel Touring au Lac
Place Numa-Droz 1
Tel: 032-725 5501
Fax: 032-725 8243
Right at the lake's edge, a few minutes' walk from the old town, this standard hotel offers good, simple accommodation and a pleasant restaurant at reasonable prices. $$

Nyon

Hostellerie du XVIe Siècle
Place Marché 2
Tel: 022-361 2441
Fax: 022-362 8566
This cosy hotel, tucked into an arcaded street in the historic centre of town, is well-situated just a few minutes' walk away from the lake and the station. $

Sierre

Terminus
Rue du Bourg 1
Tel: 027-455 1140
Fax: 027-455 2314
Terminus is right in the centre of town on the main street and a minute's walk from the railway station. It has a lively bar and terrace. $$.

Sion

Hôtel du Midi
Place du Midi 29
Tel: 027-323 1331
Fax: 027-323 6173
Reliable, centrally located. $

Hôtel de l'Ardève
Mayens-de-Chamson
Ovronnaz (16km/10 miles west of Sion)-
Tel: 027-305 2525
Fax: 027-305 2526
This delightful small three-star hotel is situated on the slopes overlooking the valley. The good hotel restaurant is open to non-residents. $$

Verbier

If you plan to stay for a week or longer, the most economical option is to rent an apartment or chalet, of which there are hundreds in Verbier. The tourist information office can supply all the details, tel: 027-775 3888, fax: 027-775 3889.

De La Poste
Rue de Médran
Tel: 027-771 6681
Fax: 027-771 3401
This medium-sized hotel enjoys a central location and offers excellent service. It has a small garden and an indoor pool. (Some rooms are expensive in high season.) $$

Zermatt

Hotel Dufour
Tel: 027-966 2400
Fax: 027-966 2401
This small, central hotel is a picture-postcard Swiss chalet. $$

Central Switzerland

Basel

Hotel Drei Könige am Rhein
Blumenrain 8
Tel: 061-260 5050
Fax: 061-260 5060
In the old town on the banks of the Rhine, this large five-star hotel has fine facilities. Ask for a riverside room. $$$

Right: Zermatt's Hotel Dufour

Hotel Rochat VCH
Petersgraben 23
Tel: 061-261 8140
Fax: 061-261 6492
Situated on the edge of the old town, this medium-sized hotel in a 19th-century building has plenty of character and a quiet location. Prices vary according to the standard of the rooms – ones without showers are available for those on tight budgets. $$.

Bern

Belle Epoque
Gerechtigkeitsgasse 18
Tel: 031-311 4336
Fax: 031-311 3936
Decorated in Art Nouveau style, and with an impressive art collection, this appealing hotel in the heart of the arcaded old town has a small bar and restaurant. $$

Innere Enge
Engestrasse 54
Tel: 031-309 6111
Fax: 031-309 6112
Located a couple of kilometres north of the old town, this delightful up-market establishment is set in peaceful gardens, and has its own jazz bar. $$$

Goldener Schlüssel
Rathausgasse 72
Tel: 031-311 0216
Fax: 031-311 5688
Good value on a quiet road off Kramgasse-Marktgasse streets. $

Brienz (for Ballenberg)

Schonëgg
Talstrasse 8
Tel: 033-951 1113
Fax: 033-951 3813
Pleasant small hotel with garden overlooking lake. Family friendly. $$

Brunnen

Weisses Rössli
Bahnhofstasse 8
Tel: 041-820 1022
Fax: 041-820 1122
This elegant little hotel has lots of character and history and a fine restaurant. $$

Interlaken

Hotel Alpina
Haupstrasse 44
Tel: 033-822 8031
Fax: 033-822 0333
A pretty family-run hotel 10 minutes' walk from the centre. Views of the Jungfrau. $

Lucerne

Pension Villa Maria
Haldenstrasse 36
Tel/Fax: 041-370 2119
A modest guesthouse on the north side of the lake, 15 minutes' walk to the town centre. $

Hotel des Balances
Weinmarkt
Tel: 041-418 2828
Fax: 041-418 2838
This lovely five-star hotel in the heart of the old town has rooms and a restaurant terrace overlooking the river. $$$

Thun

Metzgern
Rathausplatz
Tel: 033-222 2141
Fax: 033-222 2182
An atmospheric medieval inn in the heart of town. Its restaurant is recommended. $$

Eastern Switzerland

Appenzell

Hotel Taube
Marktgasse 7
Tel: 071-787 1407
Fax: 071-787 2419

Above: Bern's Belle Epoque has an impressive art collection

A traditional Appenzell house in the heart of town with modern bedrooms, and a sunny terrace for eating out in summer. $$

Bellinzona

Croce Federale
Viale Stazione 12
Tel: 091-825 1667
Fax: 091-826 2550
Old-fashioned hotel in the centre of town. Covered terrace restaurant. $

Chur

Zunfthaus zur Rebleuten
Pfistergasse 1
Tel: 081-257 1357
Fax: 081-257 1358
A beautiful 1483 mansion in the heart of the old town and full of character. Good food. $$

Locarno

Grand Hotel
Via Sempione 17
Muralto
Tel: 091-743 0282
Fax: 091-743 3013
A few minutes from the lakeside and Piazza Grande. With a pool and large garden. $$$

Camelia
Via G G Nessi 9
Muralto
Tel: 091-743 0021
Fax: 091-743 0022
Small, comfortable family hotel close to the lake and centre of town. $$

Lugano

International au Lac
Via Nassa 68
Tel: 091-922 7541
Fax: 091-922 7544
An elegant three-star hotel on the lakefront in the centre of town. Garden and pool. $$

St Moritz

Waldhaus am See
Via Dim Lej 6
Tel: 081-836 6000
Fax: 081-836 6060
Overlooking the lake, this large three-star hotel offers reasonably priced rooms, but prices rise in the high season. $$–$$$

St Gallen

Ekkehard
Rorschacherstrasse 50
Tel: 071-222 4714
Fax: 071-222 4774
Three-star hotel near the old town. Modern, comfortable rooms. $$

Schaffhausen

Promenade
Fäsenstaubstrasse 43
Tel: 052-630 7777
Fax: 052-630 7778
A pleasant medium-sized hotel in the centre of town. Caters for vegetarians. $$

Scuol

Hotel Engiadina
Rablüzza 152
Tel: 081-864 1421
Fax: 081-864 1245
Quaint hotel in the centre of the old town. $$

Stein am Rhein

Rheinfels
Rhigasse 8
Tel: 052-741 2144
Fax: 052-741 2522
This fine old building has a big restaurant terrace overlooking the Rhine. $$

Zürich

Splendid
Rosengasse 5
Tel: 01-252 5850
Fax: 01-262 6140
Small two-star hotel in the heart of the old town. Friendly, no-frills. $

Hotel Montana
Konradstrasse 39
Tel: 01-271 6900
Fax: 01-272 3070
Situated near railway, Bahnhofstrasse, and old town. Includes a highly rated French restaurant. $$

Florhof
Florhofgasse 4
Tel: 01-261 4470
Fax: 01-261 4611
Small, charming hotel near old town with lovely garden restaurant. $$$

EMERGENCIES AND HEALTH

Police: tel: 117
Ambulance: tel: 144
Fire: tel: 118
Breakdown: tel: 140

Crime is relatively rare in Switzerland but you should take sensible precautions in order to protect yourself and your property.

For medical and dental assistance, in the first instance ask at your hotel for the name of a local practitioner. In the unlikely event of drawing a blank, try Anglophone *(see Useful Telephone Numbers, page 97)*.

There are no reciprocal arrangements between Switzerland and European Union countries regarding health cover and you need to ensure you have adequate insurance as medical costs are very high. There will always be one pharmacy open out of hours in town – a notice should be pinned to pharmacy windows with details.

Most hospitals have a 24-hour accident and emergency unit.

COMMUNICATIONS AND NEWS

Post

You'll find a post office in even the smallest of villages. All except the largest city post offices close at lunchtime. There are two classes of post: A (priority), which guarantees European delivery within five days and rest of the world within 10 days; and B (non-priority) which can take up to 10 days for European destinations and eight weeks for surface-mail worldwide. The bright yellow post boxes are easy to find.

Telephones

Public telephones are very easy to come by, wherever you happen to be. Most of the country's public telephones accept both Swisscom cards (which you can purchase at post offices, newsagents and from the majority of hotels) and credit cards. Many public telephones also include a fax facility. Remember that calls made from your hotel are usually extremely expensive.

Internet Cafés

Internet or cyber-cafés can be found in the major centres; some main railway stations also have these facilities.

Media

Swiss TV has stations in German, French and Italian but airs very few quality shows. Many hotels have satellite and cable, including CNN and BBC World. Swiss Radio International broadcasts English-language news bulletins at 8am and 1.30pm. Some local radio stations such as World Radio Geneva (88.4FM) broadcast in English.

There is a plethora of local and regional newspapers; the most widely circulated are *Le Temps* from Geneva and *Neue Zürcher Zeitung* (Zürich). Foreign newspapers, including *The Herald Tribune* and most of the British papers (at about 10 times their UK price) can be found in kiosks from mid-afternoon on the day of publication (earlier at airports and major cities).

Language

There are four official languages in the country. German is spoken by 64 percent of the population in central, north and east Switzerland, French is spoken by 20 percent in the west; 8 percent speak Italian in the Ticino and less than 1 percent speak the Romansch dialects in the southeast. English is widely spoken and is becoming a second language for many Swiss. English is spoken by most people involved in the tourist and service industries.

Tours

Week-long alpine hiking, short city-breaks, two-hour city walking tours – all are easy to come by in Switzerland, or can be set up before you go. If travelling independently and in need of assistance try the local tourist office – it will have ample suggestions and itineraries. Specialist tour operators in the UK include:

- Plus Travel, 10 Wardour Street, London W1D 6QF (tel: 020-7734 0383)
- Swiss Travel Service, Bridge House, 55–59 High Road, Broxbourne, Herts EN10 7DT (tel: 01992-456123)
- Interhome, 383 Richmond Road, Twickenham TW1 2EF (tel: 020-8891 1294)

Right: enjoying life at a leisurely pace

USEFUL ADDRESSES

Swiss Travel Centre
10th Floor Swiss Court
10 Wardour Street
London W1D 6QF
Tel: 00800-100 200 30
Fax: 00800-100 200 31
E-mail: stc@stlondon.com

Swiss
Terminal 2, Departures
Heathrow
Tel: 020 8897 6511 or
London City airport
Tel: 020-7474 5747
www.swiss.com

Swiss Federal Railways
Hochschulstrasse 6
CH 3000 Bern 65
Tel: 0512-201 111
Fax: 0512-204 265
For timetable enquiries
Tel: 0900-300 300, www.rail.ch

Geneva Tourist Office
Rue du Mont-Blanc 18
Tel: 022-909 7000
Fax: 022-909 7011
www.geneva-tourism.ch

Bern Tourist Office
Tourist Center Bahnhof
Tel: 031-328 1212
Fax: 031-312 1233
www.bernetourism.ch

Zürich Tourist Office
Tourist Center Bahnhof
Tel: 01-215 4000
Fax: 01-215 4099
www.zurichtourism.ch

Useful Telephone Numbers

Anglophone (tel: 0900-576 444) is a 24-hour English-language phone service that provides information on almost all subjects, from the details of local dentists to the skiing and road conditions in a particular area.
Weather Report – tel: 162
Roads and Passes Report – tel: 163
Avalanche Bulletin – tel: 187

FURTHER READING

Insight Guide: Switzerland, Apa Publications. Updated in 2001, this edition of an award-winning series features vital up-to-date information, comprehensive references and outstanding photographs.
Fahrni, D. *An Outline History of Switzerland*, Pro Helvetica Arts Council of Switzerland.
Steinberg, J. *Why Switzerland?*, Cambridge University Press.
Style, S. *A Taste of Switzerland*. Bergli.
Harrer, H. *The White Spider*, Flamingo.
Coulson, M. *Southwards to Geneva*, Alan Sutton.
Brookner, A. *Hotel du Lac*, Penguin.
Greene, G. *Dr Fischer of Geneva*, Penguin.
Spyri, J. *Heidi*, Penguin.Mann, T. *The Magic Mountain*, Penguin.

ACKNOWLEDGEMENTS

Photography	**Jerry Dennis** *and*
46	**Kunstmuseum Basel**
63, 65	**Bill Wassman**
Cover	**Trip/W. Jacobs**
Back Cover	**Jerry Dennis**
Cartography	**Berndtson & Berndtson**

Left: sampling a Swiss lake

Insight Pocket Guide
Budapest
Sevill
Costa Del
Plus Pullout Map
Explore Your World
Discovery Channel
Practical Information
practical information

INDEX